PLAN WELL, LIVE WELL

RETIRE
READY

PLAN WELL, LIVE WELL

RETIRE
READY

JAMES R. HOLLOWAY

Published by Advantage, Charleston, South Carolina.
Member of Advantage Media Group.

ADVANTAGE is a registered trademark and the Advantage colophon is a trademark of Advantage Media Group, Inc.

Printed in the United States of America.

ISBN: 978-1-59932-453-1
LCCN: 2014958231

This publication is designed to provide accurate and authoritative information in regard to the subject matter covered. It is sold with the understanding that the publisher is not engaged in rendering legal, accounting, or other professional services. If legal advice or other expert assistance is required, the services of a competent professional person should be sought.

Advantage Media Group is proud to be a part of the Tree Neutral® program. Tree Neutral offsets the number of trees consumed in the production and printing of this book by taking proactive steps such as planting trees in direct proportion to the number of trees used to print books. To learn more about Tree Neutral, please visit www.treeneutral.com. To learn more about Advantage's commitment to being a responsible steward of the environment, please visit www.advantagefamily.com/green

Advantage Media Group is a publisher of business, self-improvement, and professional development books and online learning. We help entrepreneurs, business leaders, and professionals share their Stories, Passion, and Knowledge to help others Learn & Grow. Do you have a manuscript or book idea that you would like us to consider for publishing? Please visit advantagefamily.com or call 1.866.775.1696.

TABLE OF CONTENTS

Introduction 10

Chapter 1: Who Changed the Rules? 23

Chapter 2: Destination: Happiness 39

Chapter 3: From Acquaintance to Confidant 49

Chapter 4: When Life Happens 63

Chapter 5: So Much at Stake 77

Chapter 6: No More Paycheck! 85

Chapter 7: Portfolio Killers 95

Chapter 8: In Sickness and Health......................... 103

Chapter 9: The 401(k) Follies................................. 117

Chapter 10: At Death We Do Part 129

Conclusion: Finishing Strong 147

Appendixes... 153

Your Retirement Checklist

Important Retirement Milestones and Dates

Departing Decisions

What's Important to Me/Us

Confidential Financial Outline

ABOUT THE AUTHOR

For the past 25 years, James Sr. has helped clients to define and achieve their financial and retirement goals and dreams. His mission is to help clients create and grow wealth, protect and preserve their life savings, create a comfortable retirement income, and plan for the distribution of their estate in the most tax efficient manner.

James Sr.'s goal is for Texas Financial & Retirement to continue to be the trusted financial and retirement advisory practice and consumer advocate for Texas pre-retirees and retirees.

Texas Financial and retirement, LLC has developed a proven 3 Step Review process to help clients (1) identify their financial resources and goals, (2) clearly understand their options, and (3) select the ideal solutions for their lifestyle. This easy, efficient process is stress free and produces a written financial and retirement plan.

James Sr. has received countless civic and professional awards and is recognized as a well-known financial and retirement success educator and is an active member of the Better Business Bureau of East Texas as well as the Chamber of Commerce. With a long term track record of success, he has earned a reputation of trustworthiness, and integrity. He successfully guides clients to and through retirement and is committed to the financial success and confidence of each and every client he serves. He holds a Bachelor's degree from Stephen F. Austin University and a Masters from Our Lady of the Lake University.

James Sr. lives in Bullard with his wife Schell, and attends Bullard Southern Baptist Church. He enjoys hunting, fishing, reading, and spending time with family and friends, especially his grandchildren.

James Holloway Jr. and his wife Erin have established a successful practice with offices in East Texas and Ft. Worth, Texas. James and Erin help retirees preserve their nest egg and meet their financial goals for retirement. Specifically, they developed a proprietary 3-Step Review process – a straight-forward approach for assessing the impact of major financial decisions, while guiding clients to select the best options for their particular situation. As a dual advisor practice they can address all areas of a clients' financial and retirement needs.

James and Erin together have over 10 years of experience and reside in Arp with their two children James Lee and Kaylyn. They are active members of Grace Community Church. James Jr. serves on the Board of the Tyler Area Senior Association while Erin serves her community through involvement in Junior League. They support many local charities and organizations. James is an avid outdoors-man. Erins' interests include horses, the outdoors, gardening, and spending time on the farm with her family.

Texas Financial & Retirement LLC, Tyler Texas Office
6770 Old Jacksonville Hwy., Ste 104
Tyler, Texas 75703
903.534.5477 | 800.675.3227

Texas Financial & Retirement LLC, Longview Texas Office
2107 Courthouse Dr., Ste 102
Longview, Texas 75605
903.297.4777 | 800.675.3227

Website: texasfinancialandretirement.com
Email: bestclients@texasfinancialandretirement.com

Mission Statement
To help clients create and grow wealth, protect and preserve their life savings, create a comfortable retirement income, and plan for the distribution of their estate in the most tax effient manner.
James R. Holloway, Sr.

*I look to the future because that's where
I'm going to spend the rest of my life.*
—George Burns

INTRODUCTION

My father worked his whole career in the oil and gas business, out in the field like a lot of guys here in East Texas. When it came time to retire, the company sent him a piece of paper and told him to check one of five boxes on it. He didn't have anybody to guide him.

The top box said "single life only." Out of the five choices, that one gave him a little bit more money in his pension check each month. So he checked that box and sent it back in. Two years later, he died of colon cancer. His pension died with him.

My mom lived for 26 more years after that. I once calculated how much money that one bad decision had cost her—not even considering the lost opportunity for compounding. My best estimate was that it had cost her over $350,000.

It was a big deal in terms of the quality of her life. Instead of living comfortably, she had to be really careful with her funds. It wasn't the kind of retirement that she had envisioned. But she was lucky to have four sons and a daughter who loved her deeply. For the rest of her life, we made sure that she could support her lifestyle and do the things she wanted to do. Still, that one decision dramatically changed the quality of my mom's life and our lives forever.

The lesson is clear: The decisions you make—at the time of retirement, during retirement, and in the years beforehand—can deeply influence how well off you will be. They affect the quality of life of your family and how much you can leave to your heirs. For the retirement of your dreams, you must plan carefully.

My dad's style of planning was to hope for the best. The best didn't happen. He hadn't planned for the worst, and his decision had huge consequences for my mom. "Hope for the best but plan for the worst" is a saying that we hear a lot down here in Texas. To be able to make good decisions, you either need an advocate to help you, or you have to have enough information and education to proceed wisely.

My dad had neither. He just knew he was retiring, and if he had a choice, he wanted to get more money, not less. But those somewhat larger checks didn't come for long. There are many people out there who think the way my dad did. They're hoping for the best and they're trying their best, yet life happens.

I hear this a lot from prospective clients: "James, one of the reasons we're here to see you is that we want to do the right thing, but we're just not quite sure what that right thing is." I'm positive that is how it was with my dad. He would have done anything for his family, and I'm sure he would have done anything for my mom. He wanted to do the right thing. He just didn't know what that was.

Wisdom is not necessarily a matter of knowing. It is being able to say, "I want to do the right thing. I just need some help in figuring out what it is." No one knows it all. You defer to the people who have expertise in certain areas. They either help guide you, or they help educate you and give you the information that you need to make good decisions.

My firm, Texas Financial and Retirement, offers an array of financial services, and retirement planning is prominent among them. I have a particular passion for that because of the lesson my family learned as a result of that day my father checked a box. He worked long, hard hours his whole life. He loved his family. He had good intentions but lacked information. It might have been a good decision—if he had kept on living. But he didn't have a Plan B.

Fortunately, my mom was still in a position where she could afford necessities, and she didn't have to go back to work. She had my dad's Social Security, but she lived on a fraction of what would have been her income. That had a huge impact on her sense of freedom, financial security, and peace of mind.

I'm happy that my three brothers, my sister, and I were able to give her what I like to call the great reward. She couldn't have had that otherwise. The great reward is the freedom, after decades of work, to do what you love with the people you love for the rest of your life. She lived to 86—healthy until near the very end, when she had Alzheimer's disease—and she was deeply loved by her children and her grandchildren. Her family doted on her, and she had a good life.

Still, one of the most significant decisions affecting her life was made in a blink. My dad lacked the information and guidance to know the consequences of that decision. This happens to countless people. Their dreams for retirement don't quite work out. It's not how they envisioned those years. Along comes a day when they are dealing with grief, and the financial pressures mount. Far better if those financial matters are resolved in advance, but a lot of people fail to do so. It doesn't have to be that way.

I was only about 20 years old and in college when my dad retired. A decade later, I could have stepped forward to help him with that decision. But it was too late for that.

A BETTER WAY TO HELP

It was not too late to help others, however. When I got out of school, I went to work for what was then the Welfare Department, before it became the Department of Health and Human Services. I worked in the adult and protective services area, helping people who had not been very successful in their lives. They had all kinds of problems, from finances to health worries and more. Soon I was chosen to get an advanced degree—the state paid me while I was in school, and when I finished I returned to work for the Welfare Department for a few more years.

In that process, I decided that there had to be a better way for me to help people. In most cases, the people I'd been serving had reached a point where there wasn't much that could be done to substantially change the path of their lives.

That's why I eventually migrated to the financial and retirement side. There, I saw much more opportunity to affect the quality and the direction of people's lives. I had witnessed what was happening to so many souls, and from that experience, along with what my family had been through, I developed compassion and a drive to do something about it. I knew I could guide people through their lives in a better way.

Later, as I advanced in the Welfare Department, my duties included surveying and regulating nursing homes, so I saw that part of life, too. After leaving my position with the state, I went into the nursing home business. I owned nursing homes for about 15 years.

All through my career path, from the time I got out of school until now, I basically have served clients in the upper age range of their lives. I helped people at the Welfare Department, and helped older people who were disabled and sick and poor. Later, I progressed to regulating nursing homes, then owning them, and most recently, moved on to my career as a retirement planner, providing guidance mostly for people age 50 and older. And as a baby boomer myself, I'm right there with them in that same age group.

CROSS SECTION OF AMERICA

My clients range from 50 to 100 years old. Generally speaking, they're hardworking, independent Americans with faith and family values. They're fiscally conservative and tend to be savers.

I have a minimum asset level for accepting clients, but I don't enforce it much because a lot of my clients come to me as referrals from my existing clients. I'll usually help such referrals. I live in a very rural area, and it's not one of the more affluent communities in America. My typical clients are middle class or upper-middle class and above, although I have a wide range of clients.

I serve doctors, engineers, and other professionals, small business owners, farmers, ranchers, schoolteachers, manufacturing workers—people from all walks of life.

In other words, I serve a cross section of America. When they come to me, most of my clients are within about five years of retirement, getting ready to retire, or already retired. I've been in practice for 25 years and have clients who have been with me that long. I generally take on about 100 or so new clients a year, so I have clients coming on board all the time. These days I'm seeing quite a few baby boomers. They're much more methodical and analytical, and slower in their decision making.

Many of the folks who choose to partner up with me have previously dealt with the big national brokerage groups, the wire houses, for much of their accumulation years, and their advisors have not necessarily focused on their long-term retirement needs. I'm independent. As a matter of fact, I'm fiercely independent. I'm only beholden to my clients. I'm not beholden to somebody in New York City or St. Louis.

IN TOUCH WITH THE ISSUES

I believe in reaching out to my clients to serve them well. My philosophy is high tech and high touch. I understand the importance of having the technology tools and skills needed to solve problems and prepare for the future, but I am committed to the relationship and getting to know people one on one. I have all the research capabilities to keep pace, but I value people first and foremost. Competence is essential, but without the human touch it is cold. Nothing happens without communication. I only accept new clients if I believe we are making a commitment to serve them and their families for life.

In my part of the world, people don't judge one another by the size of their pocketbooks. I consider the guy who has landscaped my yard for 20 years to be a good friend, and yet I'm sure some of my clients have a lot more money. But his family delivers competent service, and he communicates clearly with me to make sure he knows what I want. That's what people are looking for—somebody who's got their back, who is looking out for their best interests, and also has the competence to deliver the services.

When new clients first come to see me, they bring up many concerns. If I were to distill all their concerns down to two questions, they would be: "Are we going to be okay?" and "Will my family and our resources be safe and secure?" Those who are facing the prospect of retirement want to know how to protect what they have and make sure they will continue to have enough income to support their lifestyle.

They think they're okay, but they're not sure. It's as if they want proof. Some will bring in a stack of papers and push it over to me and say, "James, we've been working for the last 40 years. We're burned out. We don't know if we can retire or not, but here's all of our stuff. Will you please tell us if we can retire, and if we can, show us how we can do it?"

It is gratifying to be able to reassure them that they can retire, but sometimes—particularly since the recent economic turbulence—I have to say, "No, I'm sorry, but you can't." I have to tell them the way it is. "Here are your choices. You need to downsize. You need to keep working." Our responsibility is to help them understand where they are.

Other questions may come tumbling out as we talk. They're also worried about whether they are going to have money for their children. Is there going to be anything left over? How do they reduce the tax bite? What about inflation?

I founded Texas Financial and Retirement about a quarter century ago, in 1989. I have offices in Tyler, Texas, and Longview, Texas. My son and daughter-in-law, James Holloway Jr. and Erin, are in practice with me, and right now we serve about 1,000 clients. We commit to lifelong relationships, and when we partner up with a family, you don't just get one advisor— you get me, you get my son, and you get my daughter-in-law. We're able to address all the financial planning needs, and of course we serve with a team of other professionals who provide special services.

A FAMILY FOCUS

We are a family practice. I am not a stockbroker, but rather an independent financial advisor, so I do have a fiduciary responsibility to my clients—a crucial distinction that I will explain in detail in Chapter 3.

When you become a client of ours, we say, "Welcome to the family." And we're not interested only in you, but also in the people you love. Our goal is to help you move successfully toward and through retirement, and that includes taking care of your spouse, your children, and your grandchildren.

We are there for you and your family, come what may, as life happens. We hold what I call family powwows, where we sit down with the folks who will either take care of business when the client is dead and gone or be beneficiaries—the trustees or the kids, for example. It's that human touch we emphasize—and we make sure we communicate thoroughly. What we've found is that clients don't know exactly what to do. Their children sometimes want to help, but they don't really know what to do either. So we explore, educate, and guide.

As we partner together, we custom design a retirement plan. We tailor it to fit the person—or to fit the family or the couple—and the only way to do that is to get to know them. Once again, it comes down to understanding that technological competence alone won't get you through to a successful retirement. The agreement with new clients is a 100 percent commitment from both sides—from my team and from the family we serve. This is important stuff.

REACHING FOR YOUR DREAMS

Every family has unique goals, dreams, values, risk tolerance, and needs. Their portfolio of assets may or may not be realistic for retirement, but as a team we help them see where they are and find out where they want to go. Then we help design a comprehensive plan to reach those unique goals.

As we go through the planning process, we aim to help them clearly articulate to themselves who they really are, where they are in life, and what they really want. Many people don't know for sure. They've never really thought much about these things, because they've been so busy with life. Other people do come in with crystal clarity about such matters—they know exactly what they want to do, whom they want to do it with, and when they want to do it. But for a lot of people, it's fuzzier than that, and we help them find some clear definitions.

Often that becomes an emotional experience for them. Sometimes they cry. They say, "I never thought of it that way." When I see the emotions, when they bring up things that are hard to talk about, I know we're getting to their core dreams. I feel reassured that we have made the human connection so necessary for progress. We're getting to the crux.

I have noticed that one of the questions I ask almost always brings an emotional response. "Bob and Mary," I will say, "I see here you have a significant portfolio. You have been very successful in your financial life. Tell me—what's the price you feel you paid for that?" And then I listen intently. The wife will look at the husband and the husband will look at the wife, and sometimes they'll both just start crying. It'll take them a minute or two to answer the question. They might never have discussed such things before, but when they start talking at this point, often they will discover the real purpose for their resources, their retirement, and their family.

I tell clients right up front, "I'm going to ask you some questions, and some of them are going to be hard questions. You're going to really have to think, because some of the questions are probably going to disturb you a little bit. I don't want you to be surprised when that happens. This is going to be a process that's going to be a little bit scary and hard at times. I want to reassure you that when we get through to the other side, you're going to be really happy you went through it."

FORWARD WITH CONFIDENCE

In this book, I will address the top concern expressed by retirees: "Will I have enough money to last the rest of my life?" I will explain how you can breathe free with an income plan designed to make sure you'll have enough to last your lifetime, and I'll show how that works. I'll offer advice on finding a good advisor and the importance of teamwork.

I'll be discussing some of the threats to your wealth: inflation, taxes, hidden fees, health care, and long-term care. These have the potential to wreck a retirement plan, but I will offer the promise of moving forward with confidence, free of fear. I'm on your side, acting in your best interest. My focus is to help you balance your risk so that you can protect your life savings while growing your portfolio enough to beat inflation and maintain something to share with the generations to come.

People typically put in 20, 30, or 40 years of their life working toward retirement, and if they don't get that right, they won't get the rewards that they dream will be theirs. They look forward to doing what they want, when they want, and with whom they want. And yet not that many Americans are living their ideal retirement. How do some people waste all those decades of hard work? It's sadly amazing.

With so much at stake, you would think that people would give retirement planning a higher priority. And yet some hardly give it a thought. Then along comes the unexpected—a sudden major illness, a market upheaval, a family crisis—and they can't handle it. Life happens, yes, and you cannot predict with certainty what will come your way, but you can plan for such events nonetheless. You don't know what the future has in store, but you certainly can prepare for what might happen. And you will breathe easier knowing that you have it covered.

CHAPTER ONE

Before you speak, listen. Before you write, think.
Before you spend, earn. Before you invest, investigate.
Before you criticize, wait.
Before you pray, forgive. Before you quit, try.
Before you retire, save. Before you die, give.
—William A. Ward

WHO CHANGED THE RULES?

In 2007, Tim and Suzanne had a million dollars in their IRA. Everything was going well for them: They were withdrawing $50,000 a year out of their account, adding it to their Social Security benefits and a small pension, and life was good.

Their plan was on autopilot, and they were enjoying retirement. They figured it made perfect sense to keep all that money in the stock market—after all, that strategy had long served them well. You pretty much know what happened next. In 2008, before they became our clients, their million dollar account went down to $500,000. But their lifestyle still depended on withdrawing $50,000.

You probably can see that they had quite a problem on their hands. They had to sell their house and substantially change their lifestyle. They spent the next four or five years trying to recoup their market losses, and by the time they became our clients they had already downsized. They lived in a smaller house, in a different town where they didn't really know anybody. They had to be much more frugal.

Tim and Suzanne's dream retirement had been snatched away from them because they had built their retirement plan not on safety and guarantees, but rather on the hope that the market would continue to move ever upward.

It's a common tale, and a sad one, of retirees finding those years to be something other than what they expected. In essence, what goes wrong is this: They don't adjust their portfolios to reflect the fact that they have become far more vulnerable to risk. They continue to invest the way they invested since they were young, when the years stretched out before them with plenty of opportunities.

This couple had built their retirement dreams on the wrong foundation. They had been fortunate to amass their million-dollar nest egg during the accumulation years of their working life. Now, in retirement, they should have been in the preservation stage—but they had not taken steps to protect their savings so that it would see them through the rest of their lives. Buffeted by an economic storm, they were too well along in years to recover. Their portfolio took a hit from which it was unlikely to recover. The retirement of their dreams had vanished.

A NEW TYPE OF RETIREE

When people first retire, they often are eager to do such things as travel or buy a motor home or take a grand cruise. Then, after they have done that, most people return to this fundamental question: "How do I spend my time with the people I love, doing the things that we can really enjoy, together?"

A few generations ago, people thought of retirement as a time for sitting on the porch and reminiscing, or walking on the beach collecting seashells. But today, the nature of retirement has changed. People travel the country, and they are highly active—from scuba diving, to motorcycling, to dance contests. Retirees are healthier and busier than ever, with plenty of energy and diverse interests, hobbies and passions.

If they have planned effectively, they have the resources to fund those activities. Most of the clients we serve have financial plans with the guarantees and certainties that allow them to go out and do those things.

Several generations ago, people of this age were on the doorsteps of death. Life expectancy was far shorter; people didn't tend to live long after their working years were done. The Social Security system was predicated on a lot of workers supporting very few retirees, who would collect benefits, on average, for only a few years. Today, the baby boomers are entering retirement at what is expected to average 10,000 a day for the next 20-plus years.

So, we're seeing an explosion of people retiring. Some have done a good job of accumulating wealth, and they're ready to enjoy their retirement years. Some are "retiring," but continue working: They're consultants in their field, or they work part time or seasonally at peak periods, or they launch new careers that are less demanding.

In short, we're seeing a wave of retirees who are retiring in different ways for different reasons. But we also are seeing a sad assortment of retirees who go back to work not because they want to, but because they need to pay the bills. They, too, had their ambitions and dreams for retirement, but for whatever reason—the economy slammed them, or they didn't plan properly, or both—they find themselves in menial jobs. Things just caught up with them.

However they fare in retirement, those thousands of new retirees each day will be putting huge demands on Social Security and on all of our benefit systems. This isn't what the 1930s-era politicians had in mind when they set up the system as a social safety net during the Great Depression. Theirs was a world where many young people could work to support a few old ones. That scenario has flipped.

ENTERING A NEW STAGE OF LIFE

For better or worse, retirement is a new stage of life—and I see many people making the transition successfully. They stay active. Their jobs and careers were not so central to their identity that they couldn't redefine themselves.

I believe that, as a society in general, we are moving away from the mindset of identifying oneself by career. Employers have been changing their company culture to adapt to the latest generation of workers, who seem to have a different attitude toward their jobs than their parents and grandparents had. At a party, for example, the first thing they ask upon meeting someone is less likely to be "So, what do you do?" They see one another as more rounded in their interests, and that's a change that I believe is affecting all of society. This makes the transition to retirement all the easier, in that people don't feel such a keen sense of loss when they no longer head into work each day.

That holds true even for professionals with whom I've worked—doctors and engineers, psychologists and craftsmen, and high-level technical people. You would think, for example, that someone who is internationally known as a drilling expert would miss that status in retirement, but I have noticed in recent years that most professionals do not. A decade ago, it was common for retirees to experience a rough transition. They didn't know what to do with themselves. Their work was their life. I've seen a huge change in that attitude. I believe that people are getting to the point where they're giving themselves permission to enjoy that "great reward."

I've also noticed that the European mindset is more relaxed. Though people there take their careers seriously, they value how much time they get off for "holiday" as much as they value the salary. They prize that time to travel and pursue other interests. I have good friends in Europe and I have good friends in South America, and they all think we're nuts here. They laugh at us.

They think, "Man, you're working hard and you're making all that money, and you're spending it on things that save you time so you can work more."

Today's retirees seem increasingly to be rounded in their approach to life. They see the time they now have available as an opportunity to do what they have long wanted to do. Some still work, yes, but many volunteer their time to worthwhile causes. In my practice, I drill down with people to see what they really like to do and how they spend their time, and I'm astonished at the diversity of their interests and hobbies and passions.

I have seen a huge growth in volunteer work, as retirees head out in great numbers to help young people. In one way or another, they want to give back. They become deeply involved in the community. They work at the food bank or volunteer to build homes for people in need. Almost all of my clients are actively involved in their church. I believe such community involvement is another reason the transition to retirement has become easier. Volunteering gets you outside yourself. When you are helping other people, you feel better. When you minister to other people's needs, you feed your own soul.

A high percentage of my clients contribute time and money in serving the community in some way. Family and faith are important to most. They do what they can to support their church and their loved ones. I think that has much to do with the essence of life.

Though my clients tend to adjust very well to this new stage of life, I know that some people do have a hard time of it. However, there are things you can do to smooth the way. An important step in retirement planning is to establish goals for the rest of your life. I've seen people get within a couple years of retirement and then scramble to save and get things into place. That doesn't work well. You need the time to make it happen.

In the last few years, when clients have sent friends to us who need help, we sometimes have had to tell those referrals that we can't do much to help them. They've lost too much, or they've planned too poorly—and often, the crux of the problem is that they've waited too long. They can point fingers where they will, but in the end they have to look closely at themselves and ask whether they were good stewards of their money. If you still have a decade or two before retirement, you can do much to turn around a troubling situation—yet far too many people postpone their planning until the brink of retirement.

"What's the very worst thing that can happen to you if you run out of money?" I often ask clients. And the most common response I hear—the most dreaded consequence—is that they would have to move in with the children. We usually laugh about it, but that's what they say. It's not that they might be homeless. It's the prospect of living with the kids. Sometimes they do say that living on the street or in their car would be the worst outcome, to which I ask: "That would be worse than moving in with your children?" Then they are quick to change their answer.

REGAINING OUR CONTROL

At educational events, I often start out by asking this question: "How many of you all agree that when those planes flew into the Twin Towers and the Pentagon, our definition of personal safety changed forever?" The response is usually unanimous. Then I'll ask: "How many people would agree that the major market downturns of the last 15 years, including the big one of 2007–2008, changed our definition of financial and retirement safety?" Again, the response is usually unanimous.

Those two major downturns—the tech bust of 1999–2000, and the recession that began several years later—woke most people up to the fact that the stock market does not go up forever and that risk is real and volatility in this new economy is the norm.

Until the tech bust, it almost had seemed that the market does go up forever. People seemed to forget the meaning of risk. Whatever they bought, whether a house or a mutual fund or a stock, the market rose. The economy seemed forgiving of people's bad decisions.

I ask a third question at these events: "Do you think the world will ever go back to the way it was? Raise your hand if you do." No one ever does. People know now that we are living in a new world economy, and that the market is not going to go up forever. "Risk is real and volatility is the norm," I say. "Would you agree?" Almost always, everyone raises a hand.

"We don't have the power individually to change the world," I say, "but we do have the power to regain control of our own destinies—and of our financial and retirement future."

A retiree can feel a loss of that control once the paychecks stop. For most people, the checks have come regularly for many years. Now, retirees have to make their own paycheck, and they can feel quite apprehensive about how to do that. Pensions, for most people, are gone, and the 401(k) and similar plans that replaced them have their own set of problems. We'll be discussing those matters later in this book.

A NEW SET OF CONCERNS

The concerns that people face in retirement are far different than the ones they faced earlier in life. "See if this sounds familiar to you," I say when speaking to a roomful of retirees or prospective retirees. "You graduated from high school and went to college. You got a real job. You started a career. You got married. You had children and saved for them to go to college. You bought a house. You made a will. Maybe you bought life insurance." I see many nods of recognition in the audience.

Throughout those years, from your 20s into your 60s, even with everything else that was going on in your life, you strived to find a way to save a portion of your earnings and grow your wealth. That was the accumulation stage of your life. Those were the days when you were building for the future and trying to pay off the mortgage. You presumed your house would gain in value and become a key part of your assets and not a liability.

And when you were younger, another huge asset was time itself. You had time on your side. You had years ahead of you to grow your assets, and you could afford to take some risks. If you make a mistake when you're young, you have decades to recover from that mistake. But when you are close to your retirement years, or in them, you may not have enough time to recover.

When you're busy advancing in your career, you get regular paychecks, with regular raises—so you don't worry about inflation as much as people on fixed incomes. The raises tend to keep pace with inflation. Meanwhile, you begin investing, often in a 401(k), and continue to add money to that portfolio. No matter what the economy is like, you're not all that deeply concerned about corrections in the market, because you are not going to be taking money out anytime soon. That money is for the long term, and you know that the market eventually is probably going to be all right—or at least, that's what we've always been told. At that age, you actually see a market correction as an opportunity, because you can buy equities at a bargain. And so you invest, each week, each month, each year, with your attention focused on getting ahead.

As you contemplate retirement, you look to see if all those years of getting ahead have gotten you far enough. The big question on most people's minds: "Will I run out of money? Have I saved enough?"

A lot of times, they just need reassurance and a plan to show them that they are going to be just fine, but they simply don't know.

A second worry, is, "Do I have enough income?" In the old economy, the general rule was, "If I can save enough money, everything is going to be okay. Then, when I retire, I'll draw my Social Security. Maybe I'll have a pension, and if I've saved enough money, I can put that in the bank." Back then, interest rates were 5, 6, 7, 8 percent or more, and if things worked out just right between your Social Security and pension and the supplemental income that you could get from your CDs at the bank, then you figured you could pay the bills, buy a new car every four or five years, maybe take a nice trip every year, and help the kids if necessary. Life was predictable and things worked out.

Now, we are in a low-interest-rate economy. Pensions are getting to be a thing of the past. The stock market is volatile and unpredictable. Things just don't work the same—the rules have changed. Even if you have a nice nest egg, the interest rates have been flat as a flitter. If you put your money in the bank, you can't depend on enough of a return to produce much supplemental income. You would have to have an awful lot of money to produce a decent income in this economy. And if you put the money in the market, you don't know if it's going to be there when you wake up.

Yet you still need to have your money work for you. You need to stay ahead of inflation, for one thing. Many people of retirement age remember the days of double-digit inflation in the 1970s, when people wore "WIN" buttons (for Whip Inflation Now) at the behest of President Gerald Ford. Though that inflation has long since been tamed, the rate historically has risen and fallen in cycles, and today the only direction it is likely to go is up. So you need your money to be making more money. You don't want it to be sitting around doing nothing. Just as you spent so many years working hard for money, you now want to send the money out to work hard for you. And you want it to come safely home at day's end.

Today's retirees experienced the recent financial earthquakes and also lived through the days of runaway inflation. They want safety and security, but they also want performance. They need to manage risk but produce income to support their lifestyle. They need to strike a wise balance if they are to be reassured that, yes, they will have enough money to last the rest of their lives.

They also need to be aware of the range of risks that await them in retirement. The cost of health care, for example, is number three on retirees' list of worries. A government study predicted that the average couple age 65 or older will now spend at least $240,000 on health care costs in retirement. That's huge. People worry about those costs and what will be covered by Medicare and whether they will need supplemental insurance. They also must face the prospect that they will need nursing home care. Without planning, that can devastate a portfolio.

Taxes, too, must be addressed in a retirement plan. "In the future, will taxes be higher or lower?" I ask retirees, and almost with one voice they expect them to rise. So, if taxes will be higher, we need to consider how to hold our assets so as to reduce the burden of taxes on them. Even though many people are in a lower tax bracket upon retirement, we need to consider that taxes are at a historic low and likely to rise. That fact has implications on whether it is wise to put so much money into tax-deferred investments, such as 401(k)s.

Another thing that people worry about is estate planning, which they start to think about once they are satisfied that they will have enough money for themselves. They wonder what they can leave to the people they love, and whether it will be their heirs or the government that gets the lion's share of that money.

More than a third of our clients list "efficient transfer of wealth" as a primary concern. They worked hard for what they have, and most believe that it will be harder than ever for their children to maintain their standard of living. They are looking for ways to pass their wealth along efficiently, with as little tax as possible, so that their children can afford a reasonable standard of living.

In this area, we have been seeing a new trend. We've always had clients wanting to efficiently transfer wealth to family and charity. But today, for the first time, parents have been setting up income planning for the kids and grandkids. They think it will become harder to produce a sufficient income, so they're not just transferring the wealth; they're using it to set up streams of income that will take care of their loved ones over time.

In upcoming chapters, we'll take a closer look at all these main concerns: health care, tax issues, and estate planning.

FROM ACCUMULATION TO PRESERVATION

In retirement, you have moved beyond the accumulation stage. You are now in the preservation stage, where your focus is on making sure you don't lose what you have gained, and that you are able to convert it into sufficient income to support your lifestyle. You are preparing now to distribute that money for your own use in retirement and, eventually, for your heirs.

The strategies of the accumulation phase may be counterproductive now. This is a time for less risk, not the same amount of risk or more. You also need to watch out for other risks, besides the market, that can derail your plan: inflation, illness, the death of a spouse, even divorce.

And you must expect the unexpected. We encourage all of our clients to have an adequate supply of liquid assets, and we want them to have a reasonable supply of emergency funds. Most people have some unexpected expenses in their lives, or they want to help loved ones who face such expenses.

The two biggest mistakes I see among folks in retirement are these: They fail to protect and preserve their assets, and they depend on unreliable investments to provide their income, both for today's bills and tomorrow's contingencies.

ONE SIZE DOESN'T FIT ALL

Sometimes I think I've seen it all in my years as an advisor, but I am still surprised by situations I've never encountered before. A lady came to see me recently who had moved from another town. She told me she was living in an extended stay hotel. "Are you looking for a house?" I asked.

She said, "Well, I was looking for a condo, and I've been looking for about six months, and I haven't found exactly what I want. So I've decided I'm just going to live at the hotel. It doesn't cost me very much. I often travel with my sister, so I'm gone a lot. People watch my belongings while I'm gone, I don't have to do any housecleaning, and they feed me two meals a day. It's gotten so that I like it there. I meet a lot of new people."

That was a new one for me. I'd never seen that before. This woman had in excess of a million dollars in investable assets. She could afford a home. "I hope you don't think I'm nuts," she said, "but I'm really very happy with my living arrangements."

It all goes to show that there are all sorts of people with unique needs and situations. As a financial advisor with a focus on retirement, I can help people sort it all out. One size doesn't fit all. People need the advice of someone who will take the time to hear about their situation.

I help people get to the truth of what is important to them; I help them identify what their life is all about. To do so, I need them to be honest with me in return. I tell clients what I think they need to hear, not necessarily what they want to hear, and I'm committed to looking out for their best interests. We talk a lot about truth and honesty. I reassure them that anything we say in this conference room stays in this conference room, and I talk about that right up front. I spend most of the first meeting getting to know who they are and what's important to them.

Usually, the more I listen and the less I talk, the better we do. Sometimes, after I've had clients for a year, I'll take them to lunch and say, "I would like for you to tell me the story of your life," and then I shut up. It's amazing how forthright they are. Each and every one of us in our lives has had a victory and tragedy, a prevailing fear, and peak moments of pride. They tell me about all of that, and we often laugh and cry together.

Almost every couple has an amazing love story. I enjoy those luncheons, because I know that in that one hour I'm going to see the intimacy between them. It's going to bond us. We'll get to the end of the hour, and they'll say, "You didn't ask us but one question, and we told you all about our whole lives." I tell them that was the point. And the next time I see them, it's like talking to old friends.

CHAPTER TWO

Alice: "Would you tell me, please, which way I ought to go from here?"
The Cat: "That depends a good deal on where you want to get to."
—from "Alice in Wonderland" by Lewis Carroll

DESTINATION: HAPPINESS

The man proudly showed me his chart. "Just take a look at what I've done here," he told me.

He and his wife were multimillionaires and were planning for retirement. He wanted to show me the extent of his savvy. They owned a motor home, and he'd done some detailed calculations. He'd compared the costs of taking his motor home on various trips versus staying in a motel, and charted out the mileages and expenses. He'd even figured in the cost of running a generator all night to heat or cool the motor home, by logging how long it typically ran in certain climates and the cost of the fuel.

This wasn't because he had to count pennies. This was because he *wanted* to count pennies.

I suppose you could argue that's how they made their millions. But for most retirees, the question should not be whether there is any way on earth you can avoid an expense. Instead, the question should be whether you can comfortably afford an expense. But the habit of saving and accumulating— a good habit, in many instances—is hard to break even when your priorities should be changing.

I recently partnered up with a doctor who had an income of about $800,000 a year and investable assets of about $6 million, plus his house. He was 63, and he and his wife wanted to retire but were afraid they didn't have enough money or income. And so they just kept working and saving money. His wife loves to travel and fears he'll die before they get to do much of that, but they keep putting things off. He has the financial ability to slow down in his career, but he's afraid. We identified options for easing into retirement in the way they had imagined it might be. There comes a time when you need to start turning a vision into a reality.

THE FEARFUL AND THE FOOLHARDY

The fear of the unknown can make people unnecessarily frugal, even when they don't need to be. I have clients who were children of the Depression or grew up poor, and remember those days with such dread that they have trouble enjoying themselves even after they have found great success. In my practice, I have met many people who have been focused so long on saving and accumulating that they have trouble adjusting to retirement. They are still growing the crop at harvest time.

On the flip side, I also deal with clients whose dreams and goals are way out of line with their financial resources. Sometimes, baby boomer couples will come in and show me that they have, say, $300,000 or $400,000 saved up, with a $100,000 or $200,000 mortgage on their home. "James, we're burned out," they say. "We need to retire. Here's what we want you to do. We want enough income to live on for the rest of our lives. For now, we want to buy a motorcycle, a motor home, and a car. We want to take three or four nice vacations a year. Oh, and by the way, we need to make sure we don't lose a penny of our money."

Now, is that possible? No. We have to do a reality check with them. In most cases, by the time we get through that process, people realize they have to downsize or keep working or save more. But sometimes they just can't grasp the situation.

I recently met with a different couple who both had quit their jobs and decided they were retiring. They didn't have an income plan; they were just living off their savings. Meanwhile, they were building a $450,000 house.

"Do you realize," I asked them, "that you really cannot afford the lifestyle that you have right now? From what I see here, you are going to need to go back to work."

"Sir," the wife said, "I've been waiting 45 years for my dream home. It's being built right now, and even if I am only able to live in it for a year or two, I'm going to have my dream home. And when it's done, even if it takes every penny, I'm going to buy the furniture for it, and all the drapes, and it's going to be just the way I see it in my mind—even if I have to be homeless one day."

In this new economy, I increasingly meet people who have gotten themselves into such a position that there's really no way out. There's not much I can do to help them, particularly when interest rates are low and the market is volatile.

I visited with a couple last year who had $148,000 in credit card debt and their income was about $80,000 a year—and how do you dig out of that? The mortgage on their house was about $3,500 a month. "How can you help us?" they asked. Good question. I had to tell them that I could walk them across the street and introduce them to a bankruptcy attorney. Maybe he could help them, but I could not. It's sad. And yet they still had dreams that they had harbored for many years about what retirement would be like. They simply didn't have the resources. They had not made good planning decisions.

I do indeed see both sides: I have talked with people who live in fear of the unknown and hunker down so frugally that they miss out on some of the joys of retirement that they could experience. And I have talked with other people who have bought into the dream but cannot afford it. They haven't planned, and so those visions will fade. Perhaps they can still make it happen if they work another two years or five years, but if they just head out and do whatever they want, it'll just be a train wreck.

At this stage of life, people's thoughts do naturally turn to whatever they imagine it means to get more out of life, whether they can afford it or not. They think about what they've always wanted to do. They've raised the kids, paid the mortgage month after month and year after year, and it's time to get on with the rest of life—whatever that might mean to them.

A VISION FOR YOUR MONEY

"What do you want this money to do for you?" I ask clients. "You worked all your life to serve your money, and now you're at the next chapter and it is going to be your money serving you. What do you want to do, and what do you want this money to do for you? How will it serve you?"

Sometimes, people can't articulate that vision, and so I might say this: "Just close your eyes for a minute and relax. I'm going to take you into the future, and you're retired. Now tell me in your mind's eye where you are, what you want to be doing, and who you want to be doing it with." Often that helps them to see the vision.

Sometimes I'll hear this: "You know what, James? I've really worked hard all my life. Here's what I want to do when I retire—nothing." And they mean it. They mean they want to do nothing for a while and rest. Usually they start talking about some plans for afterward, though.

I find out why they are retiring. Some people are retiring because they want to, some people are retiring because they have to, and some people are retiring because they have nothing else to give. They feel burned out and are jumping off the treadmill. We're seeing some of the latter in today's economy, particularly as baby boomers retire. They're just done. They may take a job, perhaps menial work, to help pay bills, but they are ready to call it quits. They'll bring in their stuff and say, "Here it is; figure out what we can do."

It seems that for some, the dream is to do nothing—at least for a while. To me, "forever" means until you get to the next place. Life is just not static, and some of the people who told me they are done for good went on to do a lot of good, indeed—they became dedicated volunteers or caregivers, sharing a lifetime of experience and wisdom. Others share that wisdom by developing a sideline as a consultant in their field. They mentor others. There are so many things that people can do. But first they need to focus enough to figure out what those things might be.

As we start out with new clients, that's a large part of what we do. At first, we just visit. I spend time just getting to know them and helping them to know themselves and what they want and need. As we visit, we decide whether we are a match. Would we enjoy partnering up with each other? Do we have the same values? Then we'll spend time getting to what I call their vision statement. What do they want their lives to look like, both now and a few years down the road? That's the heart of it.

Only then do we get into the more rational, logical side. Are the finances there to back up their vision? Is it realistic? You have to balance desire with reality. I have partnered up with many engineers. I've heard some advisors complain that engineering types are difficult to work with—"They're just so logical." But that's a good thing. I also find engineers to be emotional. You just have to keep asking the questions and listening carefully. With some clients, once you find the emotion, it just pours out—and that makes it all the easier for me to find out what matters most and to help them set priorities.

It all starts with getting to know people—letting them see that you are truly interested in them, not just trying to fix stuff. You reassure them by finding the balance between the emotional and the rational.

I tell people right up front that I'm interested in having a client for life. I want them to be looking for something besides someone to help them with an immediate problem. I want them to be looking for somebody who can help guide them through the rest of their lives, and who will help their spouse and family when they are gone.

As we plan together, it soon becomes apparent whether their goals and their dreams are realistic and can be handled by the portfolio that I see in front of me. Even if they need to switch gears, I still will help them as long as they're willing to acknowledge what they must do. I understand that people can get into a difficult spot, but blind spots are more difficult.

GETTING DOCUMENTS IN ORDER

From there, we get documents in order—and I have seen cases where those documents are scattered all over creation. Before prospective clients come in, we usually send them a packet of information about us and our process, as well as a questionnaire.

We also provide a list of everything they need to bring with them when they come to see us. Those include their legal documents, their investable assets, a statement of their 401(k) s, securities, IRAs, life insurance policies, long-term-care insurance, and a simple estimate of their budget and living expenses. We ask to see trusts, wills, powers of attorney, limited family partnerships, LLCs, and the previous year's tax return.

We make copies and organize the information into two binders with tabs. One is mine, and the other is theirs. A lot of my clients have safes and filing systems at home, and some choose to keep digital copies of their important documents as well. What's important is to be organized. It's essential to be able to get those documents easily and quickly, because someday someone else will need them. When you pass away, your loved ones may need to help settle your affairs and will need to know where to find that information. You may wish to let some people you trust know where you keep it.

Recently, I got a call from a man asking whether his brother was a client of ours. "Sir, I'm not able to tell you that. You should ask your brother," I told him, and he explained why he couldn't do that. His brother was dead. He had passed away unexpectedly. "I'm the executor of his will," he said, "and I was just calling to see if you're his advisor." So we made an appointment to get together. You never know when that day will come when others must act on your behalf, so be prepared.

Part of my job is to help people to focus and organize, whether it is those documents or their goals for the future. It's only when you can see that vision that I can effectively help plan your finances. It's hard to help people know how to best invest their money if they can't tell me what they want to do with it, or where they're going. It's better for everybody involved if we can get to the place where they can see that destination. We need to chart a course to a happy future.

CHAPTER THREE

Most people do not listen with the intent to understand;
they listen with the intent to reply.
—Stephen R. Covey

FROM ACQUAINTANCE TO CONFIDANT

The two women, mother and daughter, came in to see me with three shoeboxes that had shoestrings tied around them.

"Dad told us that if he passed away to take these three boxes to James, and he'll know what to do." I looked inside. They were packed full of bearer bonds—$340,000 worth. (They're called bearer bonds because they're payable to whoever possesses them.)

"Those boxes were sitting in the bottom of the closet for 17 years," his widow explained. He apparently had bought them with his inheritance after his mother and father died.

"You probably don't know what is in these boxes," I told them, "but it's as if you handed me $340,000 in cash."

This is an example of why you need to deal with someone you can trust in the handling of your financial affairs. For generations, financial matters in many families have been handled by the man of the house. Often the wife handled the bill paying, but the man made the financial decisions and investments. That is changing, with both spouses becoming more involved, and yet I still see many couples in which one spouse knows the details while the other seems unaware.

Every couple does a division of labor, but both spouses need to understand the financial affairs and the estate planning. If one spouse dies and the survivor has no idea about assets, resources, liability, income, and other affairs, the transition is likely to be more difficult. I still see an awful lot of that.

A POINT OF CONNECTION

When a husband and wife come to see me for the first time, I close the door and reassure them we won't be interrupted. I tell them that I'll be as alert as a first-time skydiver in a parachute packing class.

I need to know where both of them stand on the issues that will influence the rest of their lives. Most of the time, they're in the same place, but not always. I need to know what is important to them as a couple so that I can help them reach their goals. I do more than listen to what they say. I pay attention to what they're not saying. I'm listening to how they say things. I notice the glances between them.

But before we can make much progress, we need to find a point of connection. We need to communicate at a deeper level so they know that I see them as something more than a sheet of figures. If they are to become lifelong clients—and we look to someday serve their children, too, in their retirement planning—then we need to forge a relationship. And that starts with empathy. We need something we can share.

I think of my relationship with my doctor. It started with office visits for checkups and such, but it has progressed into a real friendship. I'm interested in what happens with my doctor, and he's interested in what happens with me. He knows my family, and I know his. It's a relationship far deeper than problems and solutions.

Once, during an exam, he asked me how everything was at home. I told him my mom had passed away a few months earlier. He looked into my eyes and told me his own mother also had passed away, quite unexpectedly, just a few weeks before. And we got to talking about our moms, and suddenly we both were crying. The nurse popped in and saw us sitting together on the exam table, sobbing. "Excuse me," she said, stepping backward out the door.

That was the moment of human sharing that transformed a professional relationship into something more, and it's that something more that I'm looking for in my clients.

That may be an old-school way of thinking, but it is the heart of our practice. We have the skills, resources, and technology to confidently look at all the options, explore the possibilities, and come up with a personalized solution. But we want to show our clients that we're more than just problem solvers. We reach out. We are truly interested in them and their families personally.

Sometimes, it's not a matter of just being efficient. Sometimes it takes time. It takes compassion. We have the computer programs and tools and the products—but what do those matter if they are employed without caring?

THE DIVIDENDS OF CARING

Even though we want to be efficient in taking care of our clients, I want to be inefficient with the time that I dedicate to my clients. I spend a lot of time meeting personally with them and staying in touch on the phone. We get together at special events that we arrange with them—activities both educational and fun. We send personal notes and flowers. When a client calls about an issue, I try to ease into the conversation with 5 or 10 minutes of catching up on the family. I try not to just barrel into the problem—unless, of course, it's an emergency or the client clearly is in a hurry. The human touch is reassuring.

You learn so much when you let people open up to you. It's far from time wasted. That's the way doctors should be with their patients, I believe. There are websites where you can plug in your symptoms and come up with some sort of diagnosis for yourself, with disclaimers, of course, that you need to consult with a professional. And little wonder. A good doctor gets to know the whole person, the whole patient. It's more than the charts and manuals and medications. It's more than a diagnosis and prognosis. A good doctor finds out what the patient is going through, what the changes are in his life. That's what I try to do as an advisor. If I am to serve effectively, I have to get to know the person.

In any professional relationship, a personal relationship pays dividends. For example, I recently was shopping for a used pickup truck. I found one that I liked, so I called my mechanic to find out if there were any issues with it.

"I can tell you right now, don't buy that truck, James. That was one of four bad years for that model. Don't even bring it over for me to check—it would be wasting your money and my time. So take that truck off your list—I don't want you buying it." And that was all I needed to hear. It was wise advice from a man I had come to trust. A quick phone call had saved me untold grief. Another mechanic might have grabbed the chance for a few hundred bucks just to look over a car he knew was a loser. Or, knowing I was getting a lemon that would bring lots of work his way, he might not have discouraged me from buying it. There are some mechanics like that.

You safeguard yourself by dealing with someone you know and trust. You gain security with someone who cares about you and wants to make sure you are treated right—but that means you need to develop a relationship, and that takes an investment of time.

CAN WE WORK TOGETHER?

When it comes to retirement planning, some people believe that they can do it all themselves, that they can handle their investments and they'll be just fine. I meet people like that. Often we're not a match. They come in with a two-foot-thick pile of spreadsheets about what's happened with each holding they've had for the last 30 years. I have to wonder why they are bothering with me. I ask if they have ever worked with an advisor before—and if so, how that relationship turned out, since I see they're still doing their own highly detailed analyses.

There's no shame in not knowing the best ways to invest. The problem is when you think you do but it's not at all your area of expertise. Many people are experts in one thing or another. They develop illustrious careers—but that expertise doesn't necessarily translate into investment savvy. They might not know the wise way to handle money, particularly at this critical juncture of life.

And if they do try to handle their own finances, they face information overload. People are bombarded with more information than they can sort through. They need help. If they surf the Internet, they will get an avalanche of conflicting advice, none of it personalized. The challenge is how to cut through this mass of information to get to the nuts and bolts. It's stressful just to think about, and most retirees don't relish the thought of spending their time that way. There comes a time when you want to pursue some of the things you always dreamed about.

It comes down to whether the client will ever be able to allow somebody else to help manage those funds. Some people just can't give it up. But other times, even though they did manage their own finances for years, they have gotten to the point where they lack the stamina, physically or mentally, to continue at that level of competence. One way or another, if they can concede that they need help and will accept guidance, then we can move forward.

I'll even ask the question outright: "Mr. Jones, are you willing and able to really allow me to be your financial advisor?" And I'll talk about what that means and what he has to do on his side. Sometimes I'll suggest that we each manage a portion of the assets for the first year. I call it "stick your toe in the water" financial planning. "Let's see how it goes for a year," I'll say, "and if you want to continue that way, that's fine, but if you're comfortable enough with the way I help you with your financial retirement matters, let's bring the balance into our firm." Some people find it reassuring that they haven't given up control.

I'm tailoring a plan to the individual, and a good tailor takes the measure of the man. You can't just jam people into some generic retirement plan. Each person is unique. We need to step back and have a talk with new clients, asking them about things I would never learn by just looking at their portfolio. A common pattern is that the husband wants to continue to grow the money and the wife wants to protect and preserve it. We need to find a way to reconcile those interests.

THE RACE IS NOT TO THE SWIFT

Some people walk into our office with some special issue. Basically, our job at the outset is to find out what they are afraid of. They have a "keeps-you-up-at-night" issue, as I call it. When you get to the bottom of it, for many people the issue amounts to this: "Is there going to be enough money to last?" That's often the root of their apprehensions. Related to that is: "Will our savings give us enough income to support our lifestyle?" Today's retirees are likely to live another 20 to 30 years, or more. We're seeing people today who have been retired longer than they worked.

And they face an economy that has seen a major shift from what they experienced for so many years. They've had substantial downturns in their portfolios, and they're looking for something different. They're older and wiser now, and they know it's not just about accumulating wealth. Now, it's about protecting and preserving. It doesn't do you any good to make a million dollars if you don't get to keep it. They're still looking for an above-average rate of return but don't want to spend years digging out of a hole after a downturn.

After looking at a client's investment history, I ask them to tell me about the recent downturns and how that was for them. Then I'll ask, "Do you remember the story of the tortoise and the hare?" And they relate it to me. "Tell me, then," I say, "what you see as the moral of that story." They remember that it means the slow and steady one wins the race.

And then I ask if they do any cliff diving, or skydiving, or motorcycle racing. If they have, it was years ago. "And that's because now you're older and wiser and you'd rather keep it slow and steady than rise and fall with those peaks of adrenaline. So let me ask: Would you be more comfortable now if your investments were growing slow and steady, getting above average returns without those big downturns, or would you rather just keep doing what you're doing?" At this stage of life, most prefer slow and steady. The story helps put matters in perspective.

I explain that our firm is different from many advisors, and that if they are looking to just make the highest rate of return and accumulate every penny possible by taking high risks, we're probably not a match. It's not a gunslinger economy anymore. Those days are gone, maybe forever, and most people don't expect it again in their lifetimes. They realize it will take expertise to make their money grow and avoid those downturns. We all wish we could return to those 20 or 30 boom years, when you could buy most anything and it would go up in value. But the economic world has changed.

RECOGNIZING THE RISKS

Sometimes I get new clients who are overly impressed by their nephew's investments or what their backyard neighbor is advising, even though they are at different stages of life. They seem willing to jump at whatever is touted as the latest and greatest thing. If I encounter that, I deal with it right up front.

If they feel that's the best source of advice, why are they talking with me? The advice they're getting likely is inappropriate for them, and I'll tell them so.

I had a client whose brother told her he was making money hand over fist as a day trader. "Hey, sis," he told her, "why don't you fire your advisor and give me your money and I'll make you rich." And so she fired me. Several months later, she asked if she could come back to me as a client. I asked what had happened, and she told me that in those months she had lost over $150,000.

To help people recognize the risk, I might put it like this:

"So, Mr. Jones, tell me what happened to your portfolio in 1999–2000, the tech bust?"

"It went down 50 percent," Mr. Jones says.

"And what happened to your portfolio in 2007–2008 in the big market downturn?"

"I had a million by then, but I lost 40 percent."

"So, you were down $400,000? How many years did you work, Mr. Jones?"

"40 years."

"So it took you 40 years to accumulate a million dollars, then. That means that when you lost that $400,000, you lost 16 years of your life savings." By converting the money into the years it took to save it, the risk becomes painfully clear.

"Are you willing to risk that much in the future?" I ask. And the answer, almost always, is "No."

FEES VS. COMMISSIONS

As a financial advisor, we have a fiduciary relationship, not a transactional relationship. That means we have to act in your best interests, and to place our interests below yours. I am required to do that, and it's what I would do anyway. That's the mark of a true professional.

I charge a fee for my services, based on the value of your portfolio. I prefer that to being paid to buy and sell and do transactions. If the value of your portfolio goes up and I'm charging you a fee, I make more money. But if your portfolio goes down and you lose money, I lose money, too—unlike the stockbroker, who gets his commission on every transaction regardless. I tell clients that I like being in the same boat as them. Our incentives are in alignment.

The advisor who works wholly on commissions, such as a stockbroker, is looking out for someone's interests, but not necessarily the client's interests, even though he or she might pose it that way. It is not a fiduciary relationship. For a broker, the standard is suitability: Is the recommended investment suitable—in other words, does it fit the client's objectives, time horizon, and experience? This seems reasonable, but the catch is that, among all investments that meet the suitability requirement, a broker is free to choose one that benefits them the most and the investor the least.

A good advisor will create a plan that is specific to the client's needs in one way or another. Because I have gotten to know that client, I've developed rapport and trust. I also do reviews regularly, and I track what's happening with those investments and the changes in that person's life. My clients know that I care about them and that our interests are aligned. Because I own my practice, I'm not beholden to a home office in Chicago or St. Louis or New York City.

YOU'RE STILL IN CHARGE

When you hire a good advisor, you're not losing control. You are still in charge of your money—you still have the final say—but what you are gaining is expertise. A lot of my clients are affluent because they have been astute businesspeople. If they were in charge of a company or a manager, they knew how to hand down responsibility to someone else. So why not do that now with their finances? Any good businessperson knows that nobody can do it all themselves. You have to delegate. So, why not delegate this very important responsibility to someone who is an expert in finances?

We're partners, I tell my clients, and each of us has a role. I ask whether they are willing, as a partner, to spend some time learning a bit more. We focus in large part on education. We emphasize the importance of major life decisions and how we can work together to decide the best course of action. Our job is to help you decide, based on the proper information, which option is best for you.

Through it all, emotions often are close to the surface as people talk about issues that they may not have discussed in years, if ever. When you move from being an acquaintance to being a confidant, that means that you're sharing in their life story. And sometimes, their life story has some very difficult things in it.

CHAPTER FOUR

It wasn't raining when Noah built the ark.
—George Burns

WHEN LIFE HAPPENS

Once a client and I decide to partner together, it's for life. We'll be going through a lot together. Once you get well into your 50s, the time is coming near when you will have a lot of decisions to make—including the age at which you will officially retire. You need to make sure everything is in place.

For many people, retirement is out of the picture until they reach at least 59½—the age at which they can withdraw money without a major penalty from their 401(k) or other deferred-tax retirement plan. But that alone cannot be the basis for a decision: You need to draw up budgets and work though the figures to determine whether you will have enough assets and income to move forward with confidence.

Then you will decide whether to tap into your Social Security benefits at the earliest possible time or to wait and let them grow—and, for a couple, how to coordinate that decision with your spouse's benefits. You need to make decisions about your pension, if you are one of those increasingly fewer people who have one, and about your health care arrangements.

As the years go by, you need to prepare for other life events and deadlines. For example, if you haven't been taking distributions from your 401(k), you are required to do so annually starting at age 70½, or incur a penalty. Other life events come with aging. You or your spouse could face a chronic illness, or a sudden and serious one. One of you might pass away. All these things require due consideration well in advance so that everyone is prepared.

In this chapter, I will summarize many of these life events and important dates so that you can see them on a timeline for clarity in your planning. I will go into more detail about some of them in other chapters. Here, I'll bring it all together as I do for my clients. As I develop a relationship with them, I see these issues surfacing over and over.

INTO THE RED ZONE

Life happens—and when it does, you need to be ready for it. You need to prepare for events both expected and unexpected. Most people really get serious about their preparations about five years before they expect to retire.

Some people call that the red zone, which, as any football fan knows, is when you get inside the 20-yard line. In other words, it's when you're trying to score. Most teams have what they call a red zone strategy where they change the plays. They can see the goal line. They get more intense and make some changes in their game calling as they approach. That's how it is with retirement planning: As you get closer to the goal line, you get ever more intent in your strategy.

That is when you should start switching from the accumulation phase, where you grow your wealth, to the preservation phase, where you shift your priority to protecting what you have rather than taking risks to accumulate more wealth. You can see the day is coming when you can retire.

In preparing for retirement, people get much more serious about the check-off list. They deal with questions such as these: Do we know how much our pension will be? How much will we be getting from Social Security? How much money will we have—or need—to produce supplemental income? What about the mortgage and our other debts?

At this age, you need to start thinking about that day when the last paycheck will arrive, whether from the boss, from a client, or from the proceeds of the business that you nurtured so long. That day will certainly arrive, and you will need an income stream. We need to prepare for that.

THE BROKEN STOOL

After all, the day of the pension is disappearing. If you work for a large company you may still have a pension. If you work for a government agency, you probably have a pension. Teachers, firefighters, and police have them. But for most folks, pensions are vanishing.

The trend across America has been to get out of the pension business. We've seen it with the coal companies, and we have seen it with Ford Motor Co. and numerous other companies both big and small. A lot of pension funds today are underfunded. Many companies have written people checks, and if you accept that check, you release your employer from that pension liability. For decades, people counted on those regular payouts. You worked 20, 30, or 40 years for a company, all the while expecting that pension to take care of you—and all of a sudden it doesn't exist.

It used to be common, a generation ago and more, for advisors to talk about the three-legged stool of retirement planning. You don't hear about it as much these days—and for good reason. Two of those legs are broken. The stool concept was this: You need a pension, Social Security, and personal savings—and those three, in combination, hold you up in retirement. But as we have seen, the pension leg is missing for many, and Social Security feels shaky. That stool hardly seems a stable place to rest.

As pensions began disappearing in retirement planning, employers and employees placed an increasing emphasis on 401(k)s and similar deferred-tax retirement plans. To a large extent, they replaced pensions. To invest for retirement, employees had to make contributions to those plans. In many cases, the company contributed a certain amount of matching funds.

In effect, the switch to such plans shifted retirement planning responsibility away from the employer and onto the workers' shoulders. Workers had to invest based on the financial menu of the fund—and that menu was limited. You couldn't invest anywhere you wanted. Some of the early plans required investment in the company stock. We learned, especially from Enron, that it can be very dangerous to overinvest in your company's stock. You're at the mercy of what happens to that company.

The law now allows you to move money outside of your 401(k) and invest it elsewhere. The caveat is that the law allows it, but the final decision is up to your company plan. Some permit it, and others do not.

A BREAKTHROUGH AT 59½

If you start drawing your IRA, 401(k), 403(b), or other moneys before age 59½, then not only are you taxed on the withdrawal, but you're also penalized by the government up to 10 percent on what you withdraw, except under certain circumstances.

There is a way around it called 72(t). You can be exempted if you withdraw the money in substantial equal payments over five years or until age 59½, whichever is later.

But under normal circumstances, if you don't meet certain requirements and you withdraw before age 59½ from qualified funds, IRAs, 401(k)s, 403(b)s, TSAs, and so on, then the government assesses the 10 percent penalty.

Among the first important ages to remember, then, is 59½, the age when that penalty can be avoided.

SOCIAL SECURITY MILESTONES

At age 62, another milestone arrives: That's the age when people begin to make decisions about when to start collecting Social Security benefits. You can draw benefits at age 62, if you want, but at a reduced level. Therefore, if you expect to live many more years, that might not be your best choice. It might be a good decision if for some reason you expect not to live to the usual life expectancy.

If you choose not to take the reduced benefit at age 62, and defer collecting until full retirement age, you will receive approximately a 6 percent increase each year until age 66 in most cases. After that, if you continue to postpone your benefits to age 70, then you will get about an 8 percent increase in benefits each year above the full retirement benefit amount.

The difference between electing to draw benefits at 62 versus waiting until age 70 is significant. Many of our clients delay. It makes sense to delay, especially right now, to gain that extra amount. When you add that up over the course of 30 years of retirement, you have a handsome sum of money.

Most people think there are really just a few choices—62 or 66 or 70—but married couples can have many different possible choices that most folks don't know anything about. A husband, for example, who reaches age 66 and doesn't need his benefits, could file for them and then suspend his benefits. This allows his wife to collect a spousal benefit while his own continues to accrue until age 70.

In our practice, we have a sophisticated software program that we call Social Security Maximizer. It does the calculations. You answer a three- or four-page questionnaire, and it calculates the top one, two, and three best choices for collecting the most Social Security benefits. It produces about a 14-page report that explains the different choices. For many couples, the decision can be complicated. This process goes far toward clarifying the variables and what they indicate.

A STRUGGLING SYSTEM

The Social Security system is struggling under today's demographics. In fact, the Social Security Administration has already warned us that the day is coming, in about a generation, when there will not be enough people working and paying into the system to fund benefits at 100 percent.

When the Social Security system was conceived eight decades ago, there were a lot of workers and only a few retirees, and retirees were expected to live only a few years. Today, people are living decades into retirement, and in better health. The Depression era politicians who conceived this system probably never imagined that could be the case someday.

Some people wonder whether they will need to worry, in retirement, whether the Social Security system will collapse and they will lose benefits. Here's what I usually tell them: For the baby boomer generation, Social Security benefits probably will be there for them, and probably in their entirety, although all or part of the benefits may be taxed differently. It's very unlikely, however, that our children and our grandchildren will have full benefits, and there's no guarantee for the boomers, either.

In 2032, if nothing changes, the Social Security Administration will not have the money to pay full retirement benefits, according to its own reckoning. Today's retirees may be okay, but our children and our grandchildren likely will have a much bigger problem and should not rely on Social Security for retirement.

In such an atmosphere of uncertainty, it is essential to be well informed about the available choices and the risks you could face. We help our clients move forward with the information they need to make wise decisions regarding Social Security.

HEALTH AND LONG-TERM-CARE DECISIONS

As you near retirement, you will need to start thinking about the changeover to Medicare and whether you want supplemental insurance coverage for things that it doesn't cover. This is a time when you need to also consider whether you are covered for long-term care. Most of the folks we talk with have had life experiences where they either had to take care of a parent or both parents, or had parents in assisted living or a nursing home. They know how expensive that is. Almost everybody knows someone who has gone broke because of catastrophic health care costs.

It can get even worse with the rising cost of medical care. If you're not protected against those costs, you could face dire consequences. The statistics are startling and motivating at the same time. You will read much more about these issues in Chapter 8.

Health concerns are inevitable as we age. We grow older and we die, and though that is not pleasant to contemplate, we must nonetheless plan for it. When you or your spouse becomes seriously ill, you face the prospect of needing long-term care. If someone dies, the survivor faces other issues and consequences. Statistically, it is usually the husband who dies first—and it has long been the case that husbands are more likely than wives to have pensions.

Also, because the wife often has had less pay than the husband over their lifetimes, usually the husband's Social Security benefit is larger than the wife's. The widow can elect how to receive her husband's benefit, but her own benefit disappears. She may lose the pension payments as well. That can be catastrophic for the surviving spouse, who may be unable to support their lifestyle with their new income. One of the most neglected areas of retirement planning that we see is in replacing the income of the surviving spouse.

"TAKE YOU BY THE HAND"

We have a program called "Take You by the Hand" where we help a survivor spouse, usually the widow, to address the numerous concerns that come up. We deal with such matters as Social Security and pension issues, life insurance, health care, income, expenses, and replacement income. It usually takes from a few months to even a year to get everything done. We go over a checklist and help them through a time that often feels overwhelming. It's far more efficient and comforting than what typically happens, where the widow muddles through as best she can, perhaps with the help of her children, who don't know any more than she does about what to do.

The ideal scenario is to act in advance as much as possible to avoid surprises. It is important to take the time to verify that beneficiary designations are current and in place, for example. We'll talk more about that in the estate planning chapter. But these are things that people need to keep in mind. The death of a spouse is a major life change that fully half of married people will experience. And because we can anticipate it, we can effectively plan for it.

PLANNING YOUR FUNERAL

It is also a good idea to plan your own funeral—and that, too, helps to take emotional and financial pressure off your loved ones at a very difficult time. Consider some of the elementary questions: Do you want to be buried, or do you prefer to be cremated? Do you want a religious service and rites, and if so, what would be the details of those? Do you want to preplan and prepay your funeral? Perhaps you would like to plan it in advance but not prepay. Where do you want to be buried? By the side of which loved one would you like to rest?

All those are important considerations that mean so much to people and their survivors. Funeral planning takes the burden off of your family, and in many cases it allows you to control the cost by doing it in advance. When such decisions do not need to be rendered during a time of grief, they can be made more rationally and logically.

DECIDING WHO GETS WHAT

As you approach retirement, you also need to address your wealth transfer planning decisions.

You have two choices on wealth transfer. You can take care of a significant amount of it while you're living, which very few people do, at least in our neck of the woods, or you can plan for wealth transfer at death. Of course, you can also do some combination of those.

The goal is to make sure that your heirs get the most money as efficiently as possible from a tax perspective. You want to ensure that they are getting the greatest benefit of your life's work. There are ways that you can significantly enhance the outcome by planning in advance.

I see families that are just ripped apart because the father and the mother did not make decisions about who's going to get what, when they're going to get it, how they're going to get it, and in what manner. They did not do the proper planning in terms of the transfer of wealth at death. I see it too often.

I recently met with a couple, and the wife was the executrix of her mother and father's will. She had three brothers, and none of them were speaking to her because the parents did not do proper planning for the distribution of assets in the will.

It's the kind of thing that can breed resentment, but if you clearly express your final wishes, you will spare your loved ones that stress.

MINIMUM REQUIRED DISTRIBUTIONS

Age 70½ is another important time to remember. If you have money in tax-deferred retirement plans, that's when you must begin to withdraw at a minimum schedule. That's money that has not been taxed, so it could have significant consequences for you. If you don't fulfill those minimum requirements, you could face penalties of up to 50 percent of the amount involved.

Most people are not aware of the exact age when they have to start taking those required minimum distributions. At our educational events, we ask the attendees what percentage they believe they will be required to withdraw at 70½. Very few people know. They'll guess 2 percent or 20 percent, but it's rare that even one person in a room of 20 or 30 will know what the withdrawal rate is. The actual minimum withdrawal is 3.65 percent at that age. It goes up a little bit every time you have a birthday. There's a published schedule that details the withdrawal rate.

Lots of folks don't really need those distributions. They're not living on them, and they're not spending them. They are unaware of the options they have to utilize those benefits for the survivor spouse, the children, the grandchildren, the church, or charity.

If you are not living on that money and not spending it, there are ways to put guarantees in place for the survivor spouse's income planning and to begin setting in motion efficient wealth transfer strategies. More on that in Chapter 10.

CHAPTER FIVE

*The quickest way to double your money is
to fold it over and put it back in your pocket.*
—Will Rogers

SO MUCH AT STAKE

A prospective client came to see me; he was hauling a two-foot-thick stack of statements and set them on the table.

"James," he said, "my IRA was valued at $1,080,000 back in 2007. I became a millionaire."

"Congratulations," I said. "There's a lot we could do to help you stay that way."

"Not so fast," he said. "By a year or so later, after the recession hit, I had lost a significant amount of the value of my IRA that I had worked so hard to save over the years. A million dollars was my dream." I nodded. I was sure I had heard the rest of the story before.

"I'm not a mathematician," he told me, "but I can add and subtract. Since the 2008 market downturn, I get statements every month from my stockbroker. My statement shows things like a rate of return 8 percent, 9 percent, 10 percent, etc. But I'm thinking this: I once had an IRA value of $1,080,000, and until I get back to that number, I'm not making anything. Today I have $799,000."

"That's getting better," I offered.

"I suppose," he said. "But the way I look at it, I'm pretty sure I haven't made anything until I get back to where I started."

He knew his numbers. Whether you are doing better depends on your reference point, and he knew he was still at a loss. The recession put so many people in a similar position. People lost much of their wealth. And some became shell-shocked and waited too long to get back into the market. Some have never returned to the market. In a low interest rate environment, if you weren't participating in the market rebound, it's very possible you never recovered at all.

The lesson is that unless you invest wisely and responsibly, you can have a $1,000,000 nest egg and it can be depleted to a fraction of what it was. That's particularly true if hard times come in the early years of your retirement. It can be devastating to lose money then.

Think of it as compounding in reverse. For example, if you have a million dollars in the market and the market goes down 50 percent, then you have $500,000 dollars. If the market goes back up 50 percent, you have how much money? Not a million—you have only $750,000. It takes a lot more to get back to where you were when you lose large chunks of money. You don't go down 50, then up 50 and back to where you were. It doesn't work that way. It takes much more to climb back. That's called compounding in reverse.

If the loss happens later in retirement, after quite a few good years, the consequences may not be as dire, because you will have built up your portfolio in advance. But if the bad years slam you right away, you will be struggling to climb back from that initial loss.

As far as the stockbrokers and Wall Street are concerned, though, they win regardless. Wall Street makes its money on risks—including the risks you might be taking in retirement. As you take more and more risks, however, your likelihood of success declines.

WHAT ARE YOU WILLING TO RISK?

Managing risks is at the heart of what we do. One of the techniques we use in our practice is called the Rule of 100. Generally, the Rule of 100 is this: Your age is the percentage of your portfolio that should be kept safe. Say you're 65 years old. If you subtract your age from 100, the result is how much could be kept at risk. In the case of someone 65 years old, that would be 35 percent.

When I do presentations, I explain the Rule of 100, then show people a calculation that looks like advanced trigonometry. I say, "Now, in real life, we actually go through a process more similar to this. We're just keeping it simple," and I give them a few examples. If you have no debt and a high income, then we can be more flexible with the numbers. If you have a low income, or if you have a lot of debt, or if you have a mortgage, we would adjust for that also.

We use the Rule of 100 as just one of our guidelines, tools, and techniques for managing risk in this new economy. For example, one must also carefully consider the nature of risky and safe investments. Which investments truly are in each category? The balance has often been portrayed as one between stocks and bonds. In this economy, that wouldn't necessarily be the case. Stocks and bonds are both in the world of risk, and you therefore would be exposing 100 percent of your portfolio. These days, with interest rates so low, bonds are not what you would call a fail-safe investment by any stretch. Historically, when interest rates rise, the value of bonds has fallen.

When I talk about the Rule of 100, I'm really talking about dividing your portfolio between a percentage that is kept at risk and a percentage that is not at risk at all. Remember that market downturns come regularly. If you look at a chart of market performance over the last century, or over virtually any period of time, the cycles are unmistakable. There are ups and there are downs. We need to be cognizant of that. And in major market downturns, certain sectors are not necessarily protected from the downturns. They all get dragged down.

For a quarter century or so prior to the 2008 downturn, the common advice was to "buy and hold"—just leave your money alone and don't touch it when a storm comes, because the market will always come back. After all, that always had seemed to be the case.

I think that one thing we have learned in this new economy is that risk is real. Volatility has become the norm. Instead of buying and holding, you have to manage risk carefully and be more prudent about your positions.

When talking with a couple, sometimes I will raise the point this way: "At this point in your financial and retirement life, would you rather have a plan where we could take additional risks to make you richer, or would you rather us put a plan in place that would guarantee that you'd never be poor, never run out of money?"

In a recent survey by Allianz Life Insurance Company, retirees and pre-retirees were asked whether they were more afraid of dying or running out of money. Of those responding, 67 percent indicated their greater fear was running out of money. It can be quite intimidating to think you will outlive your money. People want to protect what they have.

FINDING SAFE PLACES

As you get close to, or you are already in, retirement, you need to properly diversify so that you have an appropriate amount of your money in safe places. Diversifying helps to ensure that the money you need will not disappear. If you put a dollar in a safe place, when you come back later, that dollar will be there, or more.

Your "safe money" is money you cannot afford to lose, and you need to make sure you keep it where you can protect that principal from loss. You need an appropriate amount of safe money to support your lifestyle and pay your bills and never run out of money or income.

If you are going to have money in the risk side, you want to clearly understand that that money is at risk and have a plan, with tools and systems in place, to successfully manage or minimize that risk.

Think about a football field, with goal posts at each end. On one end is your safe money, and on the other end is your money at risk, and those ends are separated at the 50-yard line in the middle of the field. That's where you cross from safety to risk, or vice versa. I ask new clients this: "Where on the field would you want to be?" Most want their "players" to be somewhere on the safe side, so we talk about how far away from that 50-yard line they want to be. I draw a sketch of a football field, and most clients point to the goal post on the safe side. I explain that's where they would keep safe money, and we talk about inflation and devaluation of the dollar.

They point to other spots, and we talk about money markets, and CDs, and perhaps bonds. We talk about fixed index annuities and their potential to produce a yield and a reliable income stream. Clients soon realize that they want safety, but they want their players closer to the center of the field—the 50-yard line. After all, those players can move whenever needed. When we create a retirement plan, we will monitor it. Along the way, as we get from here to there, we will make a lot of little adjustments. We are not locked into the plan for the rest of our lives. We adjust the game plan as we go along.

THE RISK OF FEAR

Unrealistic fear has been one of the greatest risks to people's portfolios in recent years. That might be understandable in the wake of the recession, and yet some people have missed out entirely on a recovery. A lot of money has remained parked in low-interest accounts. Some people are so focused on what happened in the past decade that they are running scared. And when they do return to investing, they get in at the wrong time, waiting until the market is booming before jumping aboard and then selling when the market slumps. That's not caution. That's a good way to destroy wealth.

If I sense that clients are being overly cautious, I ask them to recall the story of Chicken Little, who believed the sky was falling when no such thing was happening at all. Instead, an acorn had bonked him, and it was only his own head that was hurting. Yet he thought the whole kingdom was in danger.

"It is a more difficult time," I will agree with those clients. "It is harder to do financial and retirement planning. But the world's not coming to an end—and if it were, your money wouldn't be safe anywhere. If the world were ending, there would be no reason to plan at all—we would be doomed no matter what." And that's when we look for real-world places to put their money so that it is safe and yet can work for them. Having overcome fear, they can begin to regain control over their financial future.

CHAPTER SIX

The person who doesn't know where his next dollar is coming from usually doesn't know where his last dollar went.

—Unknown

NO MORE PAYCHECK!

As you approach retirement, there comes a time when you need to put numbers on paper and find out whether and when you can take that big step. You need to determine if the figures work. A big part of retirement planning is taking the pile of money that you have gotten together through a lifetime of saving and investing and deciding the best way to turn it into an income.

Most of the people who come to see us are in pretty good shape, generally speaking, in their current situation. But when we start talking about retirement, in most cases folks are going to go from earned income to unearned income. Generally speaking, they're going to end up—even with Social Security, pensions, and so on—with less income. So, we have to build a new budget.

Occasionally, people bring in highly detailed spreadsheets, but most people just have an idea of their retirement picture and haven't really crystallized or formalized it. We'll usually start off with a balance sheet—what kind of assets and income they have, and their debts and expenses. Then we go to a current expense sheet, and then to a retirement balance sheet for expenses and income.

Sometimes, when people start looking at the figures and putting their expense and balance sheets together, they encounter some pretty big surprises. In some cases they find that they cannot retire when they wanted. In other cases, they have to change their lifestyle to make the numbers work.

People generally do not like to hear that, but somewhere along the way we have to deal with the reality of it. In some cases, people have dealt with all that up front and already know they have to downsize their house or change their lifestyle. But it's not unusual that people are caught by surprise.

For a couple, a reliable income must be in place for both of them, even after one dies. As I mentioned in Chapter 4, one area of income planning that is commonly neglected is income planning for the survivor spouse. In that area, we want to make sure that pension decisions, for example, are made correctly. If the husband has a pension and that pension dies with him, a plan must be in place so that the widow has income support. A plan must be in place to replace an income gap left by the loss of a Social Security benefit. You must ask yourself, "If something happens to me, will my spouse be secure?"—and then plan accordingly to make sure of that.

Each of us has set expenses and discretionary expenses, and for many years those expenses are covered by a regular paycheck. Come retirement, it's time to replace that paycheck. One of the things we talk about with our clients is that they need some bedrock money—money that is safe no matter what happens in the economy and that will be there to produce some guaranteed income. You don't want to play around with the money that you need every week and every month to pay your essential bills. That's your safe money—the money you cannot afford to lose. It produces the income to support your lifestyle.

INCOME STREAMS FOR DIFFERENT NEEDS

You can't play it too safe with all your money, though, because of the prospect of inflation coming back. Inflation protection is no longer built into your income as it was in your salary for so many years. You don't get those regular raises, so you have to have some growth. You need balance. You need a safe return that can still hedge against inflation, and this takes some finesse. We help the client figure out how to balance those income needs with the lifestyle that they have imagined for retirement—all those dreams they have harbored.

I help clients develop separate income streams to be used for different needs. When we are doing income planning, we are not thinking of a portfolio as one big pile of money. We break it down into separate piles for different purposes. For most of our clients, this is a new concept.

First we build an income stream just for the essentials—the mortgage, utilities, food, insurance, the basics. Then we add to that budget some of the niceties and some of the discretionary items. On top of that, we build in a plan for dealing with inflation. Right now, the government tells us we aren't having much inflation, but we know that we are in terms of gas and food. We expect inflation to be there over the years, and we usually budget it at about 3 percent a year.

NOW, LATER, NEVER

We often talk about *now* money, *later* money, and *never* money. "Now" money is money we know we're going to need right now. "Later" money is money we're going to need later on for additional expenses, such as to cover inflation and for other discretionary purchases. "Never" money is money we've squirreled away. We're not really planning on using that money unless there's an emergency or catastrophe. So it's money we're planning on never using. We're keeping it, in most cases, to pass on to the kids or the grandkids.

The reason for separating your nest egg into separate piles instead of keeping it in one lump sum is that each pile has a different function. The "now" money pays today's bills. You set aside and commit whatever amount of money that takes. That money needs to be accessible and should not be at risk.

If you have money left over after that, you can set it aside as "later" money. That would be allowed to grow to hedge against inflation, replace a car, take a vacation, give money to the kids, and so on.

If there's money left over after that, that money can go to the pile of "never" money, money that we're hoping we'll never use, although it's there for emergencies and extraordinary expenses if we need it. Generally we want to invest it in a way that allows us to pass it on to the kids or grandkids efficiently—that is, protected as much as possible from taxation.

Tax efficiency is an important consideration in designating your "now," "later," and "never" money. The "now" money might or might not be producing taxable consequences. But if you have money that you don't need right now or that you never are likely to need—your "later" or "never" money—you definitely want to position that money so that taxes are deferred or so that it will never be taxed. You should pay income tax only on the money that you're using currently. Otherwise, you're suffering consequences that you might not even be aware of.

Generally speaking, it's better to pay taxes later than sooner. That way your portfolio will have more power to grow before it is taxed. However, you also want to keep in mind the direction that you believe taxes will take in the future. Most people believe taxes will be higher—and that would be a sound assumption. If you expect higher taxes in the future, that must be figured into the value of tax deferral.

If your "now" money is exposed to the market, you can get into serious financial difficulty. As I explained previously, your portfolio—and your ability to pay for basic essentials—will take a hard hit if the market goes down at the same time that you are making those withdrawals. This system of designating portions of your portfolio to "now, later and never" will protect you from that economic mischief. You will be taking risk only to the degree that you feel comfortable and that is appropriate for the designated use of your money. You will have some very safe and protected money right up front to use for immediate needs, and you will have some less liquid money that you can tuck away to gain a better return.

A BALANCED APPROACH

In your retirement planning, you need to be aware of the concept of *liquidity*—the extent to which an investment allows you access to your money and how long you need to wait to avoid penalties. In general, growth money is less liquid than safe money. You need to keep some of your money available for immediate expenses, but you don't want to keep all of it available because that's not good investing either. If you have more available than what you need to take care of expenses, then that money is not working for you.

You need to find the balance between liquidity and growth that works for you. You want your income to be guaranteed, so you need that safe money. You need to protect that bedrock money, the nest egg money, because if you run out of money, you run out of options. But you also need growth so that you can beat inflation and meet your future income needs.

You have to have the whole picture of the years stretching out in your retirement. That's where people really tend to fall short, because most folks are not used to making budget decisions for the next 5, 10, 20 years or more. There's no formula that works for every single person. It's all up to the individual and your individual needs.

A SAFE WITHDRAWAL RATE?

It's really just a math problem. If you withdraw at too high a rate—higher than your earnings over time—you're eventually going to run out of money. When prospective clients come in, we look at what they are doing on the income side. It's not uncommon that I'll see people withdrawing at a 7 or 8 percent withdrawal rate, or even 10 percent. Yet when we examine their portfolios, they may only be earning 3 or 4 percent.

They don't seem to realize what's happening to their portfolio, but they do see that they're running out of money. No question about that—they have that part right. Maybe they have half of their money in the stock market and they're withdrawing at about a 6 or 7 percent rate of return, and they also lost 7 or 8 percent during one period. It doesn't take very long for this to have a devastating effect on their ability to create an income.

You often hear talk of what is considered a safe withdrawal rate from your portfolio in retirement. A decade or so ago, the average financial advisor would have probably said a 5 to 6 percent withdrawal rate would be safe. In the new economy, most are probably thinking of a 3 to 4 percent withdrawal rate, and even that may be too high depending on portfolio performance.

But some new studies have said the new withdrawal rate should be 2.5 percent. If you have one million dollars, that isn't a lot of income. It's sparse compared to 5 or 10 years ago. Back in the old economy, that 5 to 6 percent rate was a pretty good barometer of what you could do if you managed and budgeted your money properly. But in the new economy, with such low yields, you risk decimating your nest egg.

A TIME TO SPEND, A TIME TO GROW

There is plenty you can do to improve that situation, and I step clients through it. We take a look at income sources, how long money will be needed for particular uses, and what expenses need to be paid first. We look at a budget and discuss whether anything isn't needed. In most cases, we'll find some areas where people have expenses they don't need, such as time-shares that they haven't used in years.

This is a time to size up what you really need in life and what you don't—where the money could be falling through the cracks and where you can put it to the best use. You must always keep your goals in mind as you are setting up your income plan. You want to set aside whatever you can toward your dreams and what you hope to accomplish.

The first thing to do is make sure the essential expenses are covered, and then you can start looking at those bigger goals. The essence of effective income planning is to set priorities for how you're going to use your money, and allocate that money based on those priorities. The sooner you need the money, the less risk you can take with it. The longer it will be before the money is needed, the more risk you can take. You can expose it to the market and try to get a lot more of those gains, because you'll have more time before you have to touch it. The important thing is to not touch money that you have set aside for growth. Let that money keep growing.

What people are hoping to hear when they come to see a retirement advisor is that they will have enough money to support their lifestyle and that they will be all right. They're hoping for that feeling of relief. But hoping is not enough. The reassurance, particularly in the recent economy, comes from a formal, measurable, verifiable plan that people can see and understand. That is where they get peace of mind instead of worrying what will become of them—knowing that they have a sound retirement and income plan that will serve them well into the future and that can be adapted to fit their changing lifestyle needs.

HOW MUCH RISK CAN YOU TOLERATE?

In short, you have to try to set up an income plan so that you're taking into consideration how much risk the portfolio can tolerate, and how much risk the client as a person can tolerate emotionally and still sleep at night. The goal is to hit the target rate of return with as little risk as possible, all the while keeping in mind the intended use of that portion of your portfolio.

I recently sat down with a couple who had about $1.1 million in managed money and had a month with a $4,000 negative return. When we looked at it on a percentage basis, it was less than half a percent of a downturn in the market. Yet, they were really upset. That showed that they couldn't tolerate downturns in the market, so we did a reallocation of their portfolio.

Generally speaking, as you get older your risk tolerance goes down. Whatever plan we design has to serve long term, and therefore needs to be reviewed and modified. It must remain flexible and dynamic as we age. It's not written in stone.

It's not just the economy and the markets that change. People change, too. Their outlook and their needs change, and they may no longer feel the same way about what they want to do with their money. That's why a retirement plan needs to be readdressed regularly. You can't just tuck it away. It must be revisited, reassessed, and rebalanced.

CHAPTER SEVEN

It's clearly a budget. It's got a lot of numbers in it.
—George W. Bush

PORTFOLIO KILLERS

I often see people who once had what they felt was a sound retirement plan—back in the old economy. Interest rates were 5 to 6 percent, and they had their pensions and Social Security benefits and a nice nest egg invested in an assortment of CDs.

With all those income streams added together, it was enough for retirement, a new car, and a nice vacation now and then. They might also have felt comfortable enough to help out the kids if necessary. It was relatively simple, and it worked pretty well in the old economy.

Welcome to the new economy.

In a time of market volatility and low interest rates, many people do not have enough resources to make that plan work. They don't have a big enough retirement nest egg, yet they are too fearful to decide to do something different. They have not accepted that the old ways will no longer work for them.

Retirees are surrounded by risks that threaten their financial well-being. Those risks can be fatal to a portfolio. Besides dealing with the risk of too much market exposure—whether in stocks or in bonds—you need to consider the mischief that taxes and inflation can cause. Meanwhile, hidden fees might be munching away at your portfolio.

Even if your investments do well, you might live longer in this day and age than your portfolio is capable of serving you. One alternative to living longer is to become seriously ill—but that, too, gets highly expensive, and you may live a long time anyway, racking up costs for long-term care.

It might seem as if you just can't win, but you can. Each of those threats can be managed if you plan effectively. Let's take a closer look at each of them. If we understand what we are up against, we are far more likely to prevail.

MARKET RISK

Retirees who are invested in the stock market face the prospect of another major downturn that depletes the portfolio from which they are withdrawing an income. Just when they are hoping to claim their great reward, they suffer a blow that snatches it away. Some claim it anyway, at the very worst time, seriously compounding the problem.

There is significant risk in the bond market as well. Some people have far too much of their portfolio in bonds because they think bonds are somehow safe by definition. They need to think twice. We are living in a low-interest-rate environment. One of these days, interest rates will go up, and as interest rates go up, generally speaking, the value of the bond will go down.

As that value goes down, the bond will become less desirable. Nowadays, to get good bond rates, you have to look 10, 20, 30 years in the future. Unless you hold that bond to maturity, it is highly likely to be sold at a discount.

TAX RISK

Another threat to your portfolio is poor management of taxes. Taxes can suck away a significant portion of your assets, but there is much that we can do to reduce that bite through tax-deferred and tax-free investments. In addition, retirees face another tax hit that most people are not even aware exists. Once you begin to draw Social Security, your benefit can be taxed if your modified adjusted gross income is above a certain level. That tax hit could become greater in the years ahead as politicians seek to shore up the system. To properly plan, you need to be aware of those income thresholds so that you can minimize or possibly eliminate them.

Another tax risk actually comes from having more income than you anticipated. You no doubt have heard for years that when you retire, you should be able to withdraw funds at a lower rate because you will be in a lower tax bracket. But if you do a very good job of income planning, you may have more money coming in than you expected. You may be contributing to your own tax liability, especially if you have money that counts as income but that you aren't spending because you do not really need it.

A key component of good financial planning, and retirement planning in particular, is to find the right balance of taxable, tax-deferred, and tax-free assets. Let me emphasize again that it is a big mistake to pay taxes on money that you don't spend but just turn around and reinvest. It makes no sense, really, to do that. You should hold off as long as possible on giving Uncle Sam his cut. If you do that, you will have more money up front to put to work making more money.

Most of us pay our day-to-day living expenses with an income that is fully or partly taxable. You pay taxes on your wages, on earnings from CDs and money market accounts, and on the dividends and returns you get on most market investments.

If you have money that isn't needed for those immediate expenses—in other words, money you are not spending but may need at some later point—that's a perfect opportunity to look for tax-deferred investments. Doing so allows the money to grow and compound—you earn interest on your interest. Tax-deferred investments include your savings in a 401(k) or IRA, and tax-deferred annuities.

You may also want to look for tax-free investment options for that portion of your money that you never expect to spend and will be leaving to heirs. Tax-free assets would include tax-free bonds, Roth IRAs, and life insurance proceeds.

Whether your investments are taxable, tax deferred, or tax free will make a significant difference in the size of your portfolio over the course of 20 years. For many retirees, the major source of their retirement assets is a deferred-tax retirement plan to which they contributed for years. But that plan also can be a source of tax surprises—as we will see in Chapter 9. If necessary, you can take steps to make those plans more tax efficient.

FEE RISK

Another threat that often goes unrecognized comes from the hidden fees within mutual funds. Those fees can take away a lot of the benefits of your investment gains. There are management and a variety of other fees that can erode several percentage points from your return. You will learn about them only if you read the fund's prospectus carefully—and some you might not find even there.

It often comes as a big surprise when people realize how much of their return is being siphoned away by those fees. One of the reasons that mutual funds were invented was to allow investors, particularly small investors, to get into the market. For many people, their introduction to mutual funds came via participation in the 401(k) plan at their place of employment.

Mutual fund investors generally are at the retail expense level, with relatively high fees. Once you have gotten your portfolio up to a significant level, we generally can find ways to reduce those fees and make the cost of investing more efficient. There comes a point where mutual funds are no longer necessarily the way to go. They serve their purpose, but you can outgrow them.

The fund expenses often are called "hidden fees" because to the average investor, they are well concealed. They're disclosed in the prospectus, but I've never met anybody who has read the prospectus word for word, cover to cover. Most people flip through a couple of pages and throw it in the trash, or it gets buried in a pile somewhere. It's not most people's idea of exciting reading.

INFLATION RISK

Inflation is another serious threat, and it is a stealthy one that nibbles away at a portfolio year after year. If you don't have a plan that at least keeps pace with inflation, your standard of living is slipping a little bit each year. If you pay a dollar for a bottle of Coke this year and inflation raises that price by 3 percent next year, you will be paying $1.03. So every dollar you invest needs to earn at least 3 cents to keep up with the rising cost of Coke—or whatever else you may be buying. If your return is less than inflation, your budget gets increasingly tighter as you fail to keep up with the cost of living.

In the recent economy, we have been propping up the economy at the expense of devaluing the dollar. As I mentioned in Chapter 1, many people remember the Jimmy Carter and Gerald Ford years, with double-digit inflation and the WIN buttons that assured us we could "Whip Inflation Now." It's not beyond belief that we could return to that scenario. We're printing $80 billion a month.

We've had low inflation for years. But like the markets, inflation goes in cycles. During your working years, you probably got pay raises that kept pace with inflation. In retirement, you have to arrange for the equivalent of those raises. You do that through effective income planning that not only protects your money but provides for sufficient growth to deal with this very real threat. You can't just have your money in a mattress. You have to have a reasonable return.

Even though the inflation rate has been low lately, that won't necessarily be the case in the future, and your retirement plan must anticipate that. You are not going to beat inflation with CDs. Yes, they once commanded double-digit returns—but that was when inflation was taking an even higher double-digit toll. CDs never have kept pace with inflation. They've always been behind the curve just a little bit. So, no matter what you were getting on your CDs, you were still lagging behind inflation. And remember that the interest earned on CDs is taxable, even if you don't spend the money. You pay income tax on your earnings even if you just reinvest it into a new CD. That's not wise tax planning.

To earn a high enough return to beat inflation and other threats to your portfolio, you do need to take some element of risk with a portion of your portfolio. That's the nature of growth money. But those must always be calculated risks. You must take only the amount of risk necessary to make the numbers work to meet your needs and goals and support your lifestyle. And whenever you do accept risk, you must do so with mechanisms in place to manage or minimize that risk.

HEALTH RISK

Your retirement dreams can also be sidetracked by the cost of health care and long-term care, particularly as you get older—and having been in practice 25 years, I've seen a lot of my clients get older. If you don't plan for the costs of health care, the consequences can be catastrophic. It can devastate your life savings rapidly if you're not careful. You need a good health care and drug plan and a health savings plan. You should have long-term care and catastrophic illness protection. Most people, if they live long enough, will encounter some major health care issues. They could be chronic, debilitating, and terminal, and most involve significant expense.

If you do stay healthy and live a good long life, you face another risk—the prospect of living longer than your money lasts. Longevity risk is all too real. We all can dream of a long and hearty life. But it's also something we have to plan for. With our medical advances, some scientists are saying people may one day live to be 150 years old, and, in fact, the first person to do so may already have been born. A century ago, you were considered old in your 50s and 60s. Nowadays, many people are active in their 80s and 90s. Once, it was very rare to live to 100 years old. Now, it's common.

The risk that medical and long-term care costs can pose to your lifetime of savings is so significant and so potentially devastating that the next chapter is devoted to a detailed discussion of those matters as well as the complexities of the Medicare system.

CHAPTER EIGHT

The greatest wealth is health.
—Unknown

IN SICKNESS AND HEALTH

This chapter was contributed by Erin Holloway.

If you are like many people, you had private health insurance for years, probably provided by your employer. Then along comes retirement, and all of a sudden you get switched over to Medicare. Most people have much to learn about what Medicare offers, its costs, and the options they have once they turn 65 and become eligible.

They often don't know what is expected of them and what will be covered. Between Part A and Plan A, Part B and Plan B, Part D and drug prescription, and Part C and Plan C, it can be confusing. But once you understand it, Medicare is simple.

At age 65, most people receive a red, white, and blue Medicare card. If they're no longer working, that Medicare card will say Part A and the date when it is effective. The effective date should be the first day of the month of your birthday, so if you were born in June, you're going to get a card on June 1 of the year that you turn 65. Part A is activated by your contribution to Social Security and Medicare for 40 quarters, which means you worked and paid into the system for 10 years.

In general, Part A is hospital insurance and Part B is medical insurance. Part A covers hospital stays, surgical care, a limited amount of nursing home care, and hospice and home health services. Part B is a different part of Medicare that covers doctor bills and certain services and supplies not covered by Part A. The system has many codes for many procedures, and your doctor can help you figure out what is covered and how.

Part B is also shown on your red, white, and blue card, but it is not given to you. You get it by paying a monthly premium. In 2013 the base for that monthly premium is $104. "Base" means the minimum you will be paying for Part B. This minimum is for the average American who is retired and not on Medicaid, which has different rules. (The base can be considerably higher than $104; I've had some clients paying over $300.) The Part B premium is based on your income and has a three-year lag time; when you retire at 65 and sign up for Part B, your premium will be calculated on your income three years earlier.

Part B basically covers two types of services: medically necessary and preventive. Something that your doctor recommends that you have done every year or every six months would be considered a preventive service. Under Medicare right now, you should be paying nothing for those preventive services. Part B would also cover medically necessary services such as clinical research, ambulance services, durable medical equipment, personal hospitalization, a second opinion for surgery, or limited outpatient drugs. For example, if you are given a pain killer inside the hospital after surgery, that would also be covered by Part B.

Those who are turning 65 should determine whether they need Part B. If you are employed and have health care coverage with your employer, you may decide not to activate Part B when you turn 65. The only thing that is required when you turn 65 is that you have what we call credible coverage under a prescription drug plan, which I will explain later.

MEDICARE ADVANTAGE PLANS

Part C is called the Medicare Advantage plan, or Medicare replacement plan. There are different types of such plans, but they have a few things in common. Each Medicare Advantage plan is required to cover at least what Part A and Part B covers. You also get more benefits, including possibly some dental, some vision, some transportation, and some hearing coverage.

The Advantage plans work under contract with the federal government, which provides funding to handle beneficiaries' health care needs. The monthly premiums are low: In 2013, there were some Advantage plans with a zero premium, and some with premiums over $100.

In my opinion, these plans are best suited for people who are healthy and can't justify paying a premium for a Medicare supplement policy when they don't often go to the doctor. (Medicare supplement policies are described in the next section.) Another group of people who may choose an Advantage plan are those who can't afford the higher monthly premium for a Medicare supplement policy. Others may want an Advantage plan because they have extreme health problems and are not able to qualify for a supplement policy.

In practice, the Medicare Advantage plans are similar to major medical plans. You have a monthly premium, and you have copays and coinsurance when you go to the doctor or have procedures done. You may receive some medical bills in the mail. And a lot of people are okay with that.

Most of the Medicare Advantage plans have a prescription drug plan. It's one card and one low premium, and a lot of people like that convenience. Most of the Advantage plans are part of a network, and most require referrals: You need to go through a primary care physician to see a specialist. Many retirees were accustomed to such a system under a major medical plan.

Two of the most common types of Medicare Advantage plans are PPOs and HMOs. The PPOs, or preferred provider organizations, have a network of doctors and you pay higher copays and coinsurance if you go outside the network. The HMOs, or health maintenance organizations, have a network that you must use unless it's an emergency, or you pay the full cost of the visit.

MEDICARE SUPPLEMENTS

Medicare supplements, also called Medigap policies, supplement your original Medicare. Your original Medicare is just your Part A and Part B—that red, white, and blue card. In general terms, that card covers about 80 percent of your medical services. A Medicare supplement policy helps to fill in the gaps. You would get such a policy instead of the Medicare Advantage plan, or Part C.

Medicare supplements are plans and not parts. There are a lot of supplement plans out there. There is a Plan A all the way through Plan N. The most common is Plan F. The reason most people like to go with Plan F is because it's considered a Cadillac plan. It fills the holes in the coverage.

When you turn 65 and you don't have employer coverage, you really have two options if you want full coverage. You can have a Medicare supplement and attach a prescription drug plan to it, or you can have a Medicare Advantage plan.

There are a lot of supplement plans, and the federal government regulates what they must include. An insurance company offering Plan F must cover the exact same thing as other companies offering Plan F. What you're choosing is the company and the premium. It doesn't matter if you're on a plan with AARP, Mutual of Omaha, or another company—you're going to get the exact same coverage.

The premium prices depend on the company, of course, but when you turn 65, you can expect to pay a little over $100 per month in 2013 for a Plan F. There is no network—many people like to be free of that limitation—and you should never receive a medical bill in the mail. Many people want a Medicare supplement for the security of knowing their costs will be no more than their premium even if they spend the month in the hospital. The premiums are based on age, sex, zip code, and tobacco use. If you live in Colorado Springs, considered one of the healthier zip codes in the nation, the Medicare supplement rates are extremely low. In other areas, where people love their fried food, the premiums are higher.

PRESCRIPTION COVERAGE

The Medicare supplements do not have prescription drug coverage. You are required by law, however, to have credible coverage. If you don't have an employer plan, you need a Medicare Part D for drugs. Again, a lot of companies offer such coverage, varying by region. You cannot be declined. As long as you keep paying that monthly premium, you get the coverage.

The main considerations in a prescription drug plan besides the premium are the deductible, copays for the medication, the list of drugs covered, and the quality of the company offering the plan. Regarding the latter, it is possible for very large companies to go bankrupt. I encourage my clients to choose a company that is at least B-rated, preferably A-rated. I don't want any of them to find themselves in a position where they have to scramble to find new insurance. Although I'm confident the federal government would not make people wait until the following enrollment period, I don't want my clients to go through that stress.

All of these prescription plans have their own rules on deductibles and copays. A copay is a set amount that you're required to pay the pharmacy for each prescription drug. A deductible is the dollar amount that you have to pay out of your pocket before the insurance company will start paying for your prescription drugs.

Each plan also has its own formulary. The formulary is a list of drugs covered by a plan throughout that year. Medicare has a basic formulary that must be covered by companies offering Medicare Part D prescription plans. But most companies go beyond that basic formulary. If you are taking a specialty drug or a drug that is not often prescribed, you should make sure the drug company will cover that prescription. Formularies change, so a regular review is important. Premiums vary based on the range of prescriptions covered, as well as the amount of copay and deductible.

In our area of East Texas, the most cost-effective prescription drug plan in 2013 was $12.60 for the monthly premium. The plan has a very basic formulary, but it works well for those who are on one or two maintenance prescriptions and don't need anything else. Regarding Medicare premiums in general, people are often surprised, thinking the premiums would be higher, but don't forget that you have been paying into the Medicare system for years. I have run into a few cases where a wife has been a stay-at-home mom her entire life, and did not pay into her Part A for the required 10 years. When she turned 65, she couldn't receive Part A without paying a monthly premium. The amount of the premium depended on whether she worked at all and perhaps was just missing a few of those 40 work quarters.

It's important to understand what is known as the prescription doughnut hole, sometimes called the gap, where some people find themselves at some point over the course of the year. Think of two buckets—the insurance company's bucket and your bucket. You're on a prescription and the refill price of that prescription is $100, and your copay is $30. In 2013, when the insurance company's bucket reaches $2,750 the company says, in essence, "We did our part, we paid our limit on prescription drug plans, so now 100 percent of the cost of the prescription is your responsibility." They quit paying for prescription drugs. You are now in the doughnut hole, and you pay from your own bucket. But when your bucket reaches $4,750, you go to what we call doughnut hole coverage, or catastrophic coverage, when the insurance company steps back in to pay. Your prescriptions will then be covered at about 95 percent.

The Affordable Care Act includes measures that try to close the doughnut hole, returning 52.5 percent of the drug costs to beneficiaries. And some companies have accepted the copay even if you're in the gap, as long as you are taking a preferred generic or a generic drug.

The enrollment period doesn't allow you to change drug plans in the middle of the year, so people often ask what happens if their pharmaceutical needs change. If that happens, the drug plans will cover your new medication at least to the end of the year, when you can switch to a company that covers that drug.

MEDICARE ENROLLMENT PERIODS

When you turn 65, you can sign up for Medicare and a supplement plan, or an Advantage plan, during a seven-month period that stretches from three months before the month of your birthday to three months after. I encourage my clients to sign up early so that coverage is effective on the first day of the month of their birthday. It's usually a seamless transition.

After that initial enrollment period, there is an annual election period. Right now, that annual election period is set at October 15 to December 7, with your new policy effective January 1. For those who have moved to an Advantage plan for the first time and decided it's not what they expected, there is an additional enrollment period from January 1 to February 14, when they can move back to the original Medicare. Afterward, the plan is locked in until the next election period, unless there is a life-changing event such as job loss.

LONG-TERM CARE

Some people presume Medicare covers long-term care. But for an extended stay in a long-term care facility, the coverage just isn't there. In contrast, Medicaid does pay for the larger share of long-term care services, but of course, to qualify for Medicaid your income has to be under a certain level.

Medicare does not pay the large part of long-term care services. It doesn't help with bathing, or for supervision and custodial care. It pays for a short stay at skilled nursing facilities, hospice, and home health if you meet certain conditions: (a) you have to have had a prior hospital stay for at least three days; (b) you have to be admitted to a Medicare certified nursing facility within 30 days of your hospital stay; and (c) you must need skilled care, such as a skilled nursing facility, physical therapy, or other types of therapy to go with that. If you meet those conditions, Medicare will pay for some of the costs, but only up to 100 days.

The cost of long-term care can wipe out a retiree's life savings if they don't plan well in advance. A lot of people figure they might only need a month or so in a facility someday, so they expect to self-insure. But the average stay is now three to five years. People think they will cross that bridge when they get there, but by then it's too late. It's always best to plan ahead—to know just what you will do when you get to that bridge.

It's hard to talk about, because nobody wants to think of having to spend any time in a nursing home or being a burden to their families. But it is very important to talk to them today so that everybody understands what your wishes are and what the plan is. You can't just flip a switch over to Medicaid coverage. It doesn't work that way. To prevent your family from having financial difficulties, it's important to choose a path and stay on it. People often say they chose an insurance policy they saw online—but be sure that you know your options and that it's the right one for you. You are better off with personalized advice from a qualified advisor who cares about you and your family.

INSURING AGAINST THE COSTS

It's said that men just die, but women linger. A high proportion of those in nursing homes are women. Most families have known someone who has been in a nursing home. Once you have experienced the costs of that, you become more open to long-term care coverage. It has become much harder today for family members to be caretakers for the elderly. When my grandmother was at the end of her days, my mom was able to stay with her at home to take care of her; my grandmother was fortunate to have family nearby. That's increasingly not the case for families today, where husband and wife are both wage earners and have moved far away. I, for example, live across the country from my parents.

At the same time that medical care has extended our lives, families have become less able to care for the elderly. More people than ever are entering nursing homes, so it is critical to plan for that possibility. People have long protected themselves through traditional long-term-care insurance, but today, new products are available to help with those costs.

The commonly heard complaint against traditional insurance was that one might pay for years and never need it. "I could die in a car wreck," people say. "That's just a waste of money." And yet they will pay their auto insurance and home owners' insurance for decades without a single claim. Insurance is not to protect us against what we know will happen. It protects us against what might happen. And that's the purpose of long-term-care insurance.

Annuity products have become available for that purpose. Some life insurance companies have tried to make their product more attractive by allowing access to the funds if something catastrophic happens to the beneficiary. You can get a policy with a chronic illness or a terminal illness rider, so that you will not be penalized with surrender charges and can have access to a majority of the money in such situations.

Some of the modern life insurance policies have riders that allow money to be used to pay for nursing home costs. In some you can pull out cash value; in others, you can get cash for nursing home expenses in exchange for a reduced death benefit. We call these "living benefits," and they give some people the peace of mind of knowing that their premiums will be put to work whether they die quickly or linger in a nursing home. In the case of the former, their loved ones get the death benefit. In the case of the latter, they will have money to pay for some medical bills.

When we start talking about long-term care, people often say they are only 50 or 60 years old and won't need it for another decade or more. They are surprised to hear how much long-term care costs—and those are today's figures. Today's private room at $7,000 a month could cost $15,000 in 30 years. People fail to project forward: They may feel they could self-insure at today's rates, but what about tomorrow's? The price of long-term care has increased dramatically in the past few years as the demand for it has risen. That demand is bound to keep building, as is the need for protection against the costs. And for a married couple, that protection must extend to both. The last thing a husband wants to do is leave his spouse destitute, and that can happen if you neglect to plan.

I have a client whose wife needed long-term care a year after he retired. They had planned to travel and see the world. Instead, he paid for her care out of their own funds, and soon he was having trouble finding the payment each month. So they decided to start her on Medicaid and they had to split the estate in half. The house, the camper, the boat, and the truck were sold. He was heartbroken. Not only did she need to move to a Medicaid facility, but they lost the house that they had lived in since they were married. He now has an apartment in town and says it has all been emotionally devastating.

That kind of pain can be avoided if some advanced planning is done. There is much to consider and many pieces to the puzzle, and you will do well to get professional guidance.

CHAPTER NINE

Whoever said money can't buy happiness
simply didn't know where to go shopping.
—Bo Derek

THE 401(K) FOLLIES

I have a question," the woman on the other end of the phone said. She sounded stressed. "I'm wondering if you can tell me whether my sister has any money left in her account."

The two young women, both in their mid-20s, had inherited a sizable amount of money from their father's IRA when he passed away about 14 months previously. But because he had not arranged for any provisions to protect that money from taxes, the money went to his daughters as a lump sum, each getting an equal portion.

Along with the distribution, however, came a huge tax liability. For the year in which they received the money, each sister was obligated to pay in the highest bracket, or about a third of what they received.

"I'm sorry," I told her, "but that's private information. I can't tell you how much money she has. Why are you asking?"

"Well," she responded. "See, I've spent all my money. And now I find out I owe the IRS a ton of money and I don't know what I'm going to do. I can't pay it. I'm trying to find out if my sister has any money so I can borrow from her to pay for my taxes."

I sent her to a tax planning attorney, and I never heard from her again. That's a sad story—and, unfortunately, it's not that unusual.

A REPLACEMENT FOR PENSIONS

It has been nearly four decades since Congress added a provision to the Internal Revenue Service code that was aimed at providing a break for taxpayers. It was section 401(k), and within a few years it sprouted into the first deferred-tax savings plan by which employees could save through payroll deductions and invest for retirement. Today, such plans have become a major source of retirement income.

In fact, 401(k)s and similar plans have largely replaced the company pensions that once were a cornerstone of retirement planning. Today, not many companies provide their employees with a pension. For the most part, pensions survive only in the public sector and in some major companies.

Once, pensions provided retirees with the security of knowing that they would maintain a steady income, unless the employer went bankrupt or the pension was underfunded—not all that unusual these days. People put in years of loyal service, thinking they would have an income for the rest of their lives. It hasn't always worked out that way.

Even those companies that phased out their pensions in the 1980s must still meet obligations to those who worked for them when the plan existed—and most of those people now are retired. A lot of companies have been trying to buy out those pensions as the responsibility for assuring retirement income has shifted from the company to the employee.

The advent of 401(k)s dramatically changed how people approach their investing and retirement planning. You're not taken care of by a company anymore. You're pretty much on your own to take care of your own investments. At a recent event, I asked a roomful of 30 people how many had pensions. Four hands went up. Two of those who had pensions were schoolteachers, and one was a policeman. Those are mostly the people who have pensions now.

A WORD OF CAUTION

Even in this age of IRAs and 401(k)s, people still believe that they'll be taken care of in their retirement as long as they faithfully contribute to their accounts and choose their funds well. The way the concept has been sold to investors is that when they retire, they will be in a lower tax bracket and will be better off if they can hold off on paying taxes until then. With the additional money they retain now, they can make more on their investments.

There are two problems with that scenario. One, you may very well be in a higher tax bracket during retirement—if you do a good job in your preparations, that is. Most people would aspire to be making more money, not less. And two, the tax rate very likely will rise. You face the very real prospect of delaying today's taxes until such time as you will pay higher taxes. The tax-deferral concept looks good on paper, but in real life you must consider whether it will actually work for you.

One thing for sure is that the government is going to take its cut at some point or another. The government wants to claim its share, and a lot of tax money is sitting in those accounts waiting to be claimed. In these days of high deficits and spending pressures, the government is unlikely to shrug at such a lucrative source of revenue.

Don't get me wrong: These tax-deferred plans are indeed a systematic way to save money for future income, and to allow your money to grow all the more, since it will be exempt from immediate taxation. What's more—and this is a major benefit—a lot of companies provide matching funds, contributing a percentage for every dollar you contribute. That's a great deal. Free money is good. You can't get a much better return on your investment than free money.

A word of caution, however: Take note of what happened when Enron went bust. A lot of people lost their money because they had overinvested in the company plans. We encourage our clients to be wary of putting all of their funds into company plans. I partner up with a lot of coal mine workers who can roll over a percentage of their money outside their company plan.

We move what we can, but we also leave money behind so they can make additional contributions and get the matching funds.

There are many ways to take advantage of 401(k)s, not just for yourself but in passing it on to your heirs. In your planning, a central theme should be the likelihood that tax rates—which have been quite low by historical standards—are likely to rise. Most people expect taxes to rise and possibly get much closer to the historical average. During the Second World War and into the 1950s, the top bracket approached and topped 90 percent. In 1944–1945, the rate was 94 percent on incomes over $200,000 and 90 percent on incomes over $100,000, while the lowest bracket was 23 percent, on incomes under $2,000. Even in the 1970s, the top rate was 70 percent.

In today's low-tax climate, the direction that rates likely will go is pretty clear. The message regarding tax deferral, then, is also clear: Be careful. These plans can offer many advantages to many people. They are a principal vehicle by which most people save for retirement. Among my clients, these plans constitute one of their most valuable assets, other than perhaps their home.

TAX DEFERRAL ISN'T FOREVER

Because the government isn't going to wait forever to collect its taxes, you can't just leave your 401(k) or IRA alone in retirement without withdrawing funds. The government wants you to start using your money. You can take distributions without any penalties starting as early as age 59½. You can postpone those distributions until age 70½. At age 70½ you have to start taking required minimum distributions or be penalized up to 50 percent. The required minimum distribution today at age 70½ is currently 3.65 percent. As you get older, that minimum goes up.

I have seen people who failed to take their distributions and were penalized. And some people have several IRAs, 401(k) s, TSAs, etc. You must take the minimum distributions from all the sources. I have seen many cases where people fail to take out enough. You can take all from one source as long as you satisfy the requirement for your total required distributions. If you lose track, or don't keep up, you face a major penalty.

You won't necessarily be notified about the requirement for the distributions—and that can pose a problem, since retired people can become forgetful and face an array of other issues. This matter isn't exactly top of mind for them. Some companies will notify you that you need to take your required minimum distribution. Some companies will even tell you, based on the qualified funds, that they're holding what that distribution should be. They may even withhold the taxes, but ultimately the responsibility falls on you. Watch out for those deadlines, and keep on top of them, or make sure you are working with someone who will do that for you. The consequences can be costly.

DON'T BE TAXED TWICE

A lot of people build up substantial sums in their 401(k)s but don't need it or want it for retirement income. They would rather the money stay in the account and continue to grow. They would prefer not to have these required minimum distributions.

Some make the mistake of reinvesting those withdrawals in something else. However, remember that you have been taxed on that money, so the best use for it is to spend it. It's spending money. If you just reinvest it—say, sink it into CDs—you could end up being taxed twice. Instead, it's a good source for your income needs.

I advise clients that if they don't need the money for income—if they're not living on it—then there are other opportunities to use it well. There are ways to put that distribution, or part of it, to work to provide funds and guarantees for a surviving spouse, or for the children and grandchildren.

One example would be setting up an estate plan involving life insurance that can be paid out as a tax-free proceed. There are a number of options that will preserve your tax advantage, and the best way to learn what is right for you is to talk to an expert who can help you decide on the most efficient route.

THE ROTH IRA ALTERNATIVE

Unlike a traditional IRA, a Roth IRA gives you no tax break on the money that you put into it. You can put in $5,500 a year, or if you're over age 50, $6,500 a year if you qualify, into your Roth IRA, but you don't get a tax deduction on that money.

However, if you leave that money in for five years or longer, that money becomes tax free. All the gains it ever makes become tax free. You're not required to make distributions from the Roth in your lifetime unless you choose to. When you die, that money is a tax-free distribution to your beneficiaries.

Remember, however, that you will be penalized if you take your money out before 59½, or if you do not let those five years pass.

You can also do a Roth conversion. If you have a traditional IRA and plenty of income—that is, you anticipate you won't need the required minimum distributions for living purposes and will not be spending it—you can begin to convert that IRA into a Roth IRA. You can convert it all at once, but usually people want to avoid that huge tax liability up front and therefore convert a portion of their IRA annually over a number of years, being careful of the tax consequences. They pay the taxes on that money as it comes out of the traditional IRA and then move it into the Roth.

The concept may be easier to understand this way: Let's say I'm a farmer and I grow corn for a living. It's springtime and I go to town and I buy my seed corn. I bring it home, get out of my truck, and walk up on the porch, and there's a guy from the IRS sitting there, and he says, "Hey, James. We're here to tax you on your corn crop. Now, we're going to give you a choice. We can tax you one of two ways. We can tax you on your seed corn today [as in a Roth], or we can come back later on and we can tax you on your bountiful harvest [as in a traditional IRA]."

Which would you choose? Most people would say, "Well, we're going to choose the seed corn because there's going to be less taxable monies than the bountiful harvest."

There are many variables to consider when deciding whether a Roth conversion makes sense for you. It depends on your individual situation. For many people, it's the best way to go. Others will do better with a traditional account, maintaining their tax deferral as long as possible. Remember that with a Roth conversion, you face additional tax consequences in the year you convert. That's why people convert in increments.

TAKING YOUR LUMPS

If you should have money remaining in your deferred-tax retirement plan when you die, consider how it will be left to your heirs. Normally, unless you have made other provisions, it will be left to the designated beneficiary as a lump sum. It will be taxed according to that person's tax rate the year it is received—and that could be a high tax bracket, considering the sudden influx of all that money. It could be taxed in the 35 percent tax bracket under the current tax laws. We're talking about receiving a lump sum distribution, and for every three dollars you receive, you're giving about one dollar to Uncle Sam.

Typically, a young and inexperienced heir will not be all that concerned about Uncle Sam's dollar. That transferred wealth, which probably took the deceased person a lifetime to accumulate, can disappear in a very short time. One would hope that, unlike those sisters at the beginning of the chapter, they at least set enough aside to pay the tax obligation.

For your heirs who will receive the proceeds of a deferred-tax savings plan, you can take steps to help them avoid the big lump sum tax hit. It isn't that the beneficiary doesn't care about all that hard work you did all those years. Sometimes life just happens, and people encounter huge spending needs. All of a sudden, the sum of money is simply gone, even if they didn't spend it on a sports car.

Sometimes I'll ask clients: "Did you have a son or daughter who played some sports in high school?" Most people did. "Yeah, John played football in high school—but he didn't get a scholarship for college," I often hear.

"Well, what if Johnny would have gone from high school straight to the NFL?" I ask. "He was good in high school, but what if he'd gone straight to the pros?" People tell me things like, "He sure wouldn't have lasted long there," or "He'd have ended up in the hospital."

That's kind of what happens to young people who get inheritances. If they have not gained the experience to manage large sums of money over a longer period of time, they're probably not going to be very successful at it.

You can help them by not giving them all of the money at one time, instead setting up an income that will help them as they move through life. You can arrange a distribution that won't put the burden on them of having to make decisions about large chunks of money.

During our educational events, I'll say: "Raise your hand if you're here this evening and you'd like to leave something behind for somebody you love, but you just know they're not going to do a good job of managing that money." About half the hands will go up.

What I'll usually say to them is, "What if there was a way that you could protect those people from themselves? Raise your hand if you would be interested in learning how." They know what that means. About half the hands will go up again. Many people have somebody like that in the family.

STRETCH PROVISIONS

With deferred-tax plans, we can set up stretch provisions. Instead of giving that money to the children all at one time, we can actually stretch that money out over their life expectancy. If they're 40 years old and their life expectancy is 90, we can stretch out the distribution over a long period of time and, to a certain degree, minimize the taxes. We can put that money in a safe place where they can't lose it, and still allow it to grow and accumulate.

Then, once your children reach a level of maturity and start to see things the way you see them, they might set up a trust provision for their own children. You can also do stretch provisions for grandchildren.

Even a modest sum of money can turn into a large sum over the course of time. You can even set up the IRA stretch distribution so that your grandchildren continue to get an annual birthday check from you, for many years after you have passed on. Had you left them a lump sum, it might have been long gone by then. Instead they will get that yearly reminder that you cared about them.

CHAPTER TEN

The legacy we leave is not just in our
possessions but in the quality of our lives.
—Billy Graham

AT DEATH WE DO PART

This chapter was contributed by James Holloway Jr.

Sometimes I get into a conversation about estate planning with a client, and they tell me, "Hey, I need some of that life insurance, and I want one of those trusts."

Well, life insurance serves many purposes, and in the state of Texas there are several varieties of trusts. It's like going to a doctor and saying, "I need some medicine." You may need aspirin, or you may need Prozac.

Those tools only make sense in the context of a good plan. So I ask: "What's your plan? Are we trying to offset taxes? Are we trying to pay for college? Are we trying to ensure that your wife is going to have enough money after you pass away? Do you want to leave something to your alma mater, or a church or charity?"

A lot of people don't even really understand what estate planning is. They don't understand the dynamics of generational planning. I often say, let's just get a grasp of where you are. Assess where you're at in your estate plan. We need to figure out what we've got in place and what we don't have in place, what tools we can work with and what we can't.

UNDERSTANDING YOUR LIMITATIONS

One of our clients seems to have made it her life's mission to change her granddaughter's life. She even keeps the thermostat as low as she can to save an extra $20 for her granddaughter's benefit. That's not productive or efficient. It's taking away from her own standard of living.

You need to understand your limitations and work with the proper tools. For example, you simply may not be able to fully fund a college education. You need to be reasonable about your expectations. You may only be able to help pay for some books—and why would that not be met with gratitude?

I tell people time and time again that it is important to get a grasp of their goals. What are your goals? Once you know them, you can put your dollars to work to attain them. Every dollar we own has a job to do. I know my school fund is being taken care of. I know my retirement fund is being taken care of. I know my immediate bills fund is there. All of the dollars you have should be working, and all of the things that you do should have a goal.

Personally, I have 1-year, 5-year, 10-year, and 20-year goals—just for my personal life. That doesn't have anything to do with the estate planning that I've already started putting in place for my family. I know that I want to leave as much as possible to my children. My wife and I have set those goals and review them regularly.

It is natural and noble to want to make the biggest impact possible in your children's lives—within reason. Is your goal to make sure they will get the best education and never want for anything? Or is it reasonable to aim for something less than that? Where do you draw the line between helping and harming?

You have to create a plan. Without a plan you have nothing.

No person can build a house properly without blueprints. It can't be done. It doesn't mean that we can't adjust the plan. We can make it better and more efficient as life situations change. But you must have the foundation and framework in place first.

CHOOSE THE PROPER TOOLS

Mechanics don't work on a vehicle with nothing but a flathead screwdriver. A modern vehicle requires tools far more sophisticated than that. Nor will a level and a saw do you any good. You need the correct tools for the job. You need to keep the objective in mind.

WILLS

A will is often one of the first things people mention when they come to see us. They see a will as the means by which property will be fairly distributed to heirs so that nobody will fight. They see a will as their directive that nobody can violate.

It's not that simple. This is particularly crucial for people in a second marriage to understand. Most people do not understand that if you die and leave your assets to your spouse, your own will is finished. If each of you has children from a previous marriage, your own children can potentially be cut out because the survivor spouse attains full control. I know: It wouldn't happen to you. But I have seen it happen.

Wills serve one purpose: to settle an estate at death. Bob gets this piece. John gets that piece. Mary gets another piece. Sell this, divide that. It's very simple.

Time and time again I have heard people express the attitude that any lawyer can write a will. My family physician has a medical degree. He's highly competent, and he has "M.D." after his name. Would I want him to perform heart surgery on me? No. He's no cardiologist, and I don't think I would survive. Lawyers come in areas of expertise and specialties. For your estate plan, you should consider an attorney who specializes in elder law and/or probate. They deal with wills and trusts and powers of attorney routinely.

They can make sure you have all your wishes covered and prevent undesired and unexpected consequences.

Another important document—and one that people sometimes put off executing—is a power of attorney. Powers of attorney ensure that someone you trust can speak on your behalf whether it's a medical issue or general representation. Designating powers of attorney will keep hassles to a minimum. I also encourage people to get physician directives and have them filed electronically.

Here's a basic example of how all three of those documents work together. My grandmother on my mom's side granted power of attorney to my aunt, who lived closest to her. Eventually my grandmother needed dialysis, and she suffered a brain stem stroke. We all met at the hospital to talk about what to do, and the doctors told us her condition was irreversible. She was breathing and blinking and swallowing and that was it. My aunt had to make the decision. In her mind she saw that she was killing her mother. It took her two weeks to get past that with a lot of encouragement and a lot of love from the family and a lot of discussions with the doctor. In those two weeks a huge medical bill was amassed, and it significantly reduced the value of the estate distribution.

The second document, which works hand in glove with a power of attorney, is a physician directive. Physician directives basically tell the doctors what you want or do not want. This pre-planning can make these decisions and emotional events less traumatic.

My uncle on my father's side had power of attorney for my other grandmother, who started having mini-strokes. The doctors said her end was near. Unlike my other grandmother, my grandmother on my father's side had a physician directive. My uncle had power of attorney, and he was present, but the physician directive told the doctors what to do in my grandmother's own words. My uncle didn't have to experience the guilt that my aunt went through. My grandmother's wishes were clear.

TRUSTS

Trusts, as I said, come in many shapes and forms and do many different things. Some trusts are built specifically to protect special needs children. Some trusts are built to protect gun ownership.

Whatever the situation is in a family, there will be a specific tool to work perfectly in a trust. Think about how many people live on your street, how many people you work with, and how many people you go to church with. Now, out of all those people, how many have the exact same medication list as you, in the exact same dosage as you, and take it at the exact same prescribed time of day as you? More than likely, the answer is none. With the trust, because there are so many of them that do so many very specific things, we have to make sure that (a) we're getting the right one, and (b) it is implemented correctly.

I can't tell you how many times I've seen people with a trust that may not be the one they need. It has not been funded or built correctly. Once the legal documents are formed, they haven't done anything past that. Why spend the $2,000 to $5,000 to have the thing built if you're not going to use it? You have to follow through to make sure that the trust is enacted in the way you desire.

WEALTH TRANSFER VIA ROTHS

Roth IRAs, as discussed in Chapter 9, can be excellent tools for transitioning wealth. Not only do you not pay taxes on it if you keep the money in the account for five years or until you are 59½, whichever is later, but neither do your beneficiaries. You can convert a traditional IRA into a Roth IRA, but you have to pay income tax on the amount converted in the year that you do so. In other words, you can marry Mr. Roth, but you have to pay the dowry. And then you have to wait at least five years and do everything he says.

GIFTING

Gifting is one of the most underutilized aspects of long-term estate planning. The rules of gifting change, but, in general, it can be used in specific ways to change the lives of your children or grandchildren. For example, you can give little Mary, age 7, money through the Uniform Gift to Minors Act. However, you remain in control of that money, not the child's parents, and certainly not Mary. The money grows and grows, in a safe place for her education. If she decides, at 17, to go to college, you can put it into an account where she cannot access most of it. The account can be set up to pay out twice a year, before spring and fall semester. To avoid crazy spending, you can require her mom's or dad's signature to sign off on the account. From the time Mary is a little girl and all the way through her college years, you maintain full control of that gift.

That's impactful. Such gifting is efficient and life changing, yet seldom used. Plus, the money remains in a safe place. If you want to change your grandchild's life, why would you put that money in a risk position and potentially lose it all? Safe money places are very important in forward legacy planning. You must abide by specific rules on taking out the money early, but the principal is protected from loss.

LIFE INSURANCE

"I'm just not interested in buying any of that life insurance stuff," I often hear. But it is the most efficient, effective tool that exists today for growth. Not only are the proceeds tax free, but in almost every single case I have helped design, a fraction of a percent of the overall estate is able to massively amplify what the heirs receive.

Nowhere else can you do the math and see that you will be able to produce an annualized gain of 12 to 17 percent over the rest of your life and then have it pay out to your heirs free of taxes. That is monumental. No investment opportunity exists to produce earnings annualized at that high a level. As we saw in Chapter 8, modern life insurance can also include some living benefits, helping to cover end-of-life expenses, such as nursing home costs—and that function, too, can be a huge benefit to the estate.

SPOUSAL PLANNING

Sometimes when I bring up the subject of spousal planning, clients will cock their heads as if puzzled. One man told me,

"Well, she's right here. She's going to bury me and then have fun with the rest of the money." That may be the case. But before that, you have a lot to figure out.

First, you need to think about the potential for nursing home and end-of-life expenses. That is the number one destroyer of estates. Statistically, a husband and wife can anticipate spending $200,000 or more on health insurance coverage and health insurance expenses after age 65.

The bulk of that comes at the very end. The average American has a 67 percent chance of going into a nursing home, and the average stay is 2.5 years. That's $120 a day, or $43,000 a year. That's $109,000 per person for the average stay. For a couple, that's $200,000-plus spent. That can devastate an estate, and severely diminish a surviving spouse's lifestyle. Through proper planning and long-term-care coverage, you can protect against that.

Spousal planning must also take a look at the potential loss of Social Security benefits. The Social Security Administration says that the average survivor spouse will lose $1,008 a month of income just in Social Security. The average survivor spouse, typically the wife, will live 7–12 years past her spouse. If 10 years is typical, that's about $120,000 in income lost over the remainder of her life. Here's the question that you must ask yourself: Is that loss going to change my standard of living? Often, the answer is yes.

In addition, if your spouse is receiving a pension, we need to know how that works, and we need to calculate what the loss of income will be if pension benefits stop or are reduced at death. The survivor spouse doesn't want to come up short. That's no way to live.

In planning for income and transition of wealth for a survivor spouse, you also need to consider such things as re-titling the home and property. You should get expert help in guiding you through that. The ladies at the bridge table don't tend to talk about such matters. There's no "Idiot's Guidebook to Losing a Spouse." You need to find out in advance about such matters as Social Security benefits and pension rollovers. You need to be prepared, for example, if a funeral director pulls you aside and says, "Hey, if your loved one had life insurance, just bring in the policy and we'll take care of getting these funeral expenses paid and you can just relax." But the funeral home may also tack on an additional service charge. Ask if there is a surcharge, and if there is, just go directly to the life insurer for the proceeds.

There are many such matters that we want to make sure are addressed correctly. You cannot leave anything to chance. We have seen serious issues arise, and you must act sooner rather than later on getting all of these things changed. You do not want to try to deal with these matters when you are grieving. Your mind needs to be clear so that you can make the best decisions. An emotional decision is unlikely to serve you well.

CHARITABLE GIVING

The Lord said to tithe 10 percent. That's what I've been taught my whole life, and I believe, as Anne Frank pointed out, that "no one has ever become poor by giving."

Many people have tax-deferred investments that will realize taxes upon their death, and often they wish to leave additional money to their place of worship. Unless that transfer is structured correctly, however, it might not happen. If you're going to give money to the church or to anybody, first make sure that the recipient knows about it. It needs to be written down. It needs to be framed so that your wishes are taken care of.

There are a couple of different ways that you can work with the church to get your estate moved over or a portion of your estate moved over. Most institutions work with a charity or specialist in such matters or can recommend one to you. In a church, we want to talk to the elders, or the pastor, or whoever is in charge of those types of decisions. We want to make sure that everyone is on the same page on the amount of proceeds and the structure. You may want the church—or any charity—to have only a portion of the estate and you may want it directed for specific purposes, and if so, it must be listed and titled that way. It all needs to be planned in advance.

One of my favorite clients was a military chaplain—a fighting man, but a godly man. His objective was to have $1,000,000 saved to build a business wing at his alma mater. We hit the mark, and I asked about the plans moving forward. Did he want to institute this before he died, or after? He hadn't thought that far ahead. So, we met with a counselor for the college and started discussing everything. The proceeds would be transferred upon his death to the college. He was very specific about how he wanted everything done. He wanted to make a significant difference in people's lives through his plan to give back.

We also can set up scholarship funds or very specific purchasing options for schools and colleges. Things of that nature can truly change people's lives. They can make huge impacts in our communities and on our society. Those are excellent ways of giving back.

One caution that I mention to clients involves volunteer organizations. A lot of them are regional, based in a specific community, and typically they do not have money managers. Once we pass away, we want to have a team in place that can help us to manage that and get the funds to the volunteer organization. You do not want to hand over large chunks of money to a volunteer organization. Typically that money is spent quicker and may not provide maximum benefit to the organization. We want to be constrictive on how such a group receives and uses this gift.

AVOIDING DEBT FOR YOUR HEIRS

AT-HOME CARE

People who are able to stay in their own homes tend to live longer, and at-home nursing care can be a big help. But that costs money and requires proper planning.

You can get at-home health care through multiple tools, including long-term-care policies and hybrid annuities. You can get life insurance with living benefits built into it. A lot of dual-purpose tools can provide the service.

What we don't want to do is eat away at your estate to pay for it so that you have less to give. It currently can cost $75,000 for a year of at-home nursing care before entering a facility. That means that almost $300,000 of an estate, if not planned properly, typically can evaporate.

To avoid that, you must have the pieces in place to protect yourself, to protect your spouse, and to protect your heirs.

FUNERAL COSTS

Nationally, the average cost of a funeral is approximately $8,500. Many funeral costs are well above that figure and costs will probably increase in the future. Plan for inflation.

There are a number of ways to pay for a funeral or cremation. You can get a funeral trust, or you can self-fund. You can also purchase a funeral plan through a pre-need plan or through a final expense insurance plan.

You need to be careful when you purchase a funeral plan. Take time to verify that your purchase is with an established, reputable company and that these benefits will actually be available for some time in the future. Be sure you know exactly what services your plan will and will not cover. Don't forget you will also need a plot (two plots if you have a spouse).

Prearrange your plans with as much specificity and detail as you desire. This will be a welcomed burden off your loved ones' shoulders. Make sure your spouse, loved ones, and/or the funeral home have a written copy.

MEDICAID PLANNING

To help protect the survivor spouse from becoming destitute, you can also explore Medicaid planning. This is how it works: When you are considering a nursing home, you will be asked to list your assets, their value, and their location. I've had clients tell me that they've been asked how much gold their mother had, and how much a piece of property was worth.

This is done to discover your assets, and you must comply with a five-year "look-back" rule. To be eligible for Medicaid coverage in a nursing home, you can have a maximum of $14,400 in countable resources. Certain assets, such as the home and retirement accounts, might be exempt. If you give money away in the five years before applying to enter a nursing home, the government assumes you did so to qualify for coverage. Earlier gifts will not affect your eligibility.

Let's say that four years previously you gave your grandson $10,000. You can be required to return that $10,000 for use toward your nursing home costs. Medicaid planning can help to circumvent some of that, but it's very tricky and you should never attempt it on your own. You need a specialist in that field. We have a couple of Medicaid planning specialists who work closely with us. They help structure the estate to protect as much of it as possible through proper Medicaid planning. Volumes of books could be written on Medicaid planning, full of advice on doing it correctly and horror stories about how it was messed up. But your individual situation needs the attention of a specialist.

EDUCATE YOUR HEIRS

The average inheritance in the United States is spent in 14 to 17 months. Have you worked that hard saving, growing, and sacrificing to build your estate for it to be spent so quickly? To avoid that, it helps to prepare your heirs for the day they will receive your estate. That is rarely done, but those who do it well can transform their families.

There's an old saying, "Shirtsleeve to shirtsleeve in three generations." Most people have heard it, but they're not sure what it means. It is saying this: The first generation didn't have much. They worked really, really hard, saved and scrimped, and did everything they could to better the next generation. Those in the next generation spent some of the money, and they worked. But they weren't on the factory line; they were up in the office, or white collar. But, because of how the estate was managed and how the estate had been structured by the first generation, by the time you get to the end of the life of the third generation, they're back to working on the factory line as blue collar workers. The estate has basically been dismantled. It's gone. That is the behavior you want to break. If you can stop that behavior, if you can educate your family, you will transform your family's future.

You need to have family meetings. I tell our clients, "No surprises." You sit down with an intermediary, typically the person who is helping you move all these pieces into place, and you honestly and openly talk to everybody who is going to get something. Explain to them: Here's what I have, and here's how it's going to work. They need to know the what, the when, and the how. If they don't, do you think they're going to be very respectful of the money when they get it? I have observed that almost every time those facts are kept from loved ones, the money is spent very quickly.

Educate, educate, educate. I cannot stress this enough. Give them articles to read. Talk about it at holiday gatherings or while visiting on the back porch. Talk about it to your grandchildren. Talk about how you want everybody's lives transformed. Send them good material to read and understand. Ask your advisor for good reading material and videos to give to your family.

The more your loved ones know, the more they understand, the more they truly see that you are attempting to transform their lives and their children's lives and the next generation's lives, the higher the probability of breaking the shirtsleeve to shirtsleeve cycle. If you're paying for little Susie's college, she needs to know that, and she needs to understand how it happens. I love it when clients bring their grandkids in and we discuss money concepts. The kids actually get into it: "Wow, really granddad, you're doing this for me?"

One client told me that once she started these family meetings, and everybody really got on the same page and saw that she was trying to change their world, the love poured out. They saw how much she cared, and they returned that caring. "They started doing things for me to help change my life," she told me. Sometimes it just takes that first spark, starting with a family meeting.

I also encourage families to create a family mission statement: This is who you are, these are your family goals for the next generation. Talk about it at Thanksgiving and at Christmas. You can truly make life-changing differences in your family.

When I talk about such matters, people often comment: "That's fine for some, but I'm not a Carnegie or a Rockefeller or a Kennedy. I don't have that much money." I ask them to get a calculator and run the numbers.

Let's say you have a $500,000 life insurance policy, with your two children as beneficiaries. Just considering that alone— not to mention the rest of your estate—each child will get $250,000. Let's say they each keep $100,000 and put the other $150,000 into a new life insurance policy that will pay out $2,500,000 to your two grandchildren. They get $1,250,000 each. They keep $750,000 and put the remainder back into a life insurance policy. Your money turns into $7 million in three generations. It does not take much to revolutionize a family. You may not be a Carnegie, and you may not be a Rockefeller, but with a very little bit of work and a specific resource to fit your situation, you can transform your family.

Every situation is different. Do not accept a cookie cutter plan. Have a specified detailed plan built for your situation. Remember, with proper planning, it is possible that your wishes can be achieved. Proverbs 10:4 states, "A slack hand causes poverty, but the hand of the diligent makes rich." If we do nothing or put little effort into planning, the rewards will be few.

CONCLUSION

FINISHING STRONG

This should be abundantly clear to you: It's not your mom and dad's retirement anymore.

No longer do people work and save and sacrifice and then retire to rock on the front porch or walk on the beach picking up seashells. Nowadays people expect more from their retirement years. And more and more, the responsibility for a comfortable retirement falls on the retiree, not the company for which he or she labored.

The world is becoming increasingly complicated and moving at an ever faster pace. We are a part of a new global economy where volatility is the norm, and we now understand risk is real.

There is a tremendous amount of information out there about retirement planning, but it has become so voluminous and complex—and at times contradictory—that it is becoming more difficult to gather what is pertinent and make wise decisions to reach your retirement dreams.

I deal with people who are, in most respects, very sophisticated and very intelligent, and who have achieved various degrees of financial success. That sophistication doesn't always translate into financial sophistication, however.

It's really kind of mind-boggling. The superintendent of a large public school system once asked me, "Can you tell me how to make a balance sheet?" Now that's scary.

And a lot of people have a built-in resistance to financial matters. For whatever reason, they just don't want to deal with it, they don't consider it fun, and they don't consider it anything but drudgery. Yet, if they don't give it proper attention, they can really hurt themselves. Again, that's why you don't have to do it alone. You just have to find someone to guide you. You have to find someone you can trust and partner with that person and not be afraid to say, "Explain these concepts to me because I don't understand them."

It can feel overwhelming, and it can be daunting. Most people don't have the time or the inclination to really learn very much about financial affairs beyond the basics of deposits, paying bills, and putting a little bit into retirement plans. Many people just struggle with those basic concepts.

It is wise to seek professional help, someone who not only can advise you but also educate you along the way. Someone who can help you translate, to take concepts from the complex to the simple. You need an advocate who can guide you on the path to and through retirement. You have spent a career developing the skills that led to your success—but those skills don't necessarily include the financial sophistication needed to thrive in retirement so that you make the most of your nest egg for you and your heirs.

When it comes to financial and retirement planning, you do want to be in control of your money. You want to understand what you're doing, and you want to be educated and informed enough that you can make prudent decisions.

But you don't have to know everything. You can flip a light switch without knowing the intricacies of how electricity works. If you see sparks or hear sizzling, it's time to bring in an electrician. I don't know what my doctor knows, but I do know how much I need his expertise. I know when I feel the symptoms that indicate I need a professional.

I hear this comment often: "James, we know we need to do something, but we don't know exactly what we need to do. Can you help us figure out what we need to do?" That moment of need arises in virtually everyone's financial life, and those who are wise will defer to the experience of people who have seen situations similar to yours many times. You are not giving up control over your finances, any more than you are ceding authority over your health and safety when you call that doctor or that electrician. The very act of seeking assistance shows that you are acting responsibly. You care about yourself and your family.

I often tell folks when I look at their assets, "You all need to be very proud of what you've accomplished. You have accumulated a very valuable estate here." In many cases they'll have no debt. We can fine-tune the details, but they deserve to be proud of what they have accomplished.

In the approach to retirement, you are nearing the end of the accumulation phase of your financial life. You found the pot of gold. You perhaps worked effectively for years with an advisor who helped you in the accumulation phase. And now you are entering a new phase—a time when you must preserve what you have gained and prepare to distribute it. You need to turn it into a reliable income and create a legacy for loved ones.

The tactics and strategies that helped you accumulate all this wealth won't necessarily be the areas to which you need to give the utmost attention in this next phase of your financial life. You have planted and cultivated, and now it is harvest time.

In this new season, you still want to put some of your money to work making more money, but the emphasis overall must shift to protecting it. You don't want to take the kinds of risks that you may have taken when you were young. You need to stay ahead of inflation, but you need to make sure you have a reliable income for the next 10, 20, 30 years or more—and not just for you, but for your surviving spouse. And when both of you are gone, how will you efficiently transfer that money to your children, your grandchildren, your church, or your charity?

Our purpose in the past was working to accumulate wealth. Now our purpose is putting our wealth to work for us, so that we can accomplish our goals and dreams. We move onward to our great reward, for ourselves and our loved ones and our communities—and we prepare to finish strong.

SPECIAL BONUS

I have included several additional complimentary documents and tools in the appendix to help you discover and guide you on your financial and retirement journey. These guides will help you define where you are on your journey, the resources you have accumulated, and where you want to go in your financial and retirement future. If we can be of help, please contact us at one of the following:

(phone)   903.534.5477

(phone)   800.657.3227

(email)   bestclients@texasfinancialandretirement.com

(web)   www.texasfinancialandretirement.com

God Bless!

APPENDIXES

Your Retirement Checklist

Important Retirement Milestones and Dates

Departing Decisions

What's Important to Me/Us

Confidential Financial Outline

YOUR RETIREMENT CHECKLIST

The average marriage lasts about eight years according to the U.S. Census Bureau. A typical job lasts about 5 years according to Forbes Magazine. And according to the social Security Administration, the average American is retired for over 20 years.

One of the most important decisions of your life is deciding when and where to retire. Do not retire without completing this retirement checklist.

1. **Decide what you want to do in retirement–define your lifestyle.** Maybe you want to do more gardening, play more golf, or travel. But most retirees look beyond themselves to set real-life goals, whether it is starting their own business, writing a family history, traveling to all seven continents or taking care of their grandchildren.

2. **Define your target date for retirement.** This will help you stay on track and help your decision plan remain on schedule

3. **Do you want or need to work?** According to a recent survey, three quarters of today's workers expect to work part time after they retire. But only about one quarter of retirees actually do so. If you plan to work after retirement, explore your options ahead of time.

4. **Decide where you will live.** The majority of retirees never leave home. Some move, some downsize, and some relocate closer to grandchildren.

5. **Figure out your health insurance and health care cost.** Obama Care (The Affordable Care Act) will definitely change our cost and expectations about healthcare. Much is still unknown and the phase-in will make decisions more difficult.

6. **Take inventory of your assets.** The main difference between working and retirement is you no longer get a paycheck in retirement. You should take a realistic picture of your financial assets, including pensions, social security and retirement accounts, and all other resources to see if you have the resources to support yourself for 20 or 30 years. Factor in debts and inflation.

7. **Determine where your retirement income will come from.** You must turn your assets into the stream of income to pay your bills. Add up your monthly income from pensions, Social Security and any other sources. Then figure out how you're going to produce income from your retirement accounts and personal savings. It can be a complicated process, consult a professional for assistance.

8. **Decide when to sign up for Social Security.** Conventional wisdom says you receive full benefits once you hit full retirement age, which is 66 for most of us. Benefits are reduced at age 62 and will increase up to age 70. Retirement planning experts can help you maximize those benefits.

9. **Consider long-term care/assisted living.** There is a 50 percent chance that today's 65-year-old couple could live past the age of 90. Consider long-term care insurance as a possible solution.

10. **Plan for unexpected expenses.** You will incur unexpected expenses such as medical, home repair, replacement

costs, etc. Set aside at least 10% in your budget for those unexpected expenses.

11. **Consult and communicate with your spouse.** Start well before retirement to define common ground with your spouse on likes/dislikes, personal and collective vision of your retirement future. Remember change can be scary but exciting when planned well.

12. **Make a plan.** This is the most important step you must take. Many pre-retirees fail to take the time to develop a written plan. A written plan will help you evaluate your success. Be specific, but allow for flexibility and change. Now get ready to live and enjoy the retirement of your dream; the big reward.

IMPORTANT RETIREMENT MILESTONES AND DATES

In order to maximize your retirement benefits you'll need to circle a few important dates on your calendar. Do not miss these important retirement milestones!

AGE 50

Workers age 50 and better can start making catch-up contributions to many retirement plans such as the 401(k), 403(b), and governmental 457(b). In 2014, a worker who is 50 or older can contribute a total of $23,000 into one of these plans which is a whopping $5,500 above the limit that workers age 49 and under are eligible to save. Likewise, workers 50 and older can contribute an additional $1,000 into their individual retirement accounts, or IRAs, for a total contribution of $6,500 annually. Eligible workers can also make $2,500 additional catch-up contribution to their SIMPLE IRA or SIMPLE 401(K). Capitalize on these growing limits so that you can maximize your tax deferrals or tax exemptions (depending on whether your accounts are structured as traditional or Roth accounts (respectively). Furthermore, retiring police medics, and firefighters can take penalty-free distributions from their plans starting at age 50 if they've completed at least 20 years of service.

AGE 55

This is the earliest age at which you can withdraw money from your 401(k) without paying the 10% early withdrawal penalty if you are no longer in that position and quit after reaching 55. But please note you can only withdraw the funds from the 401(k) associated with your most recent employer. You cannot withdraw money from your IRA just yet.

AGE 59 ½

You can now withdraw money from your IRA without paying the 10% early withdrawal penalty. You can also withdraw money from any 401(k) account, but it must be the retirement account associated with the job you most recently left.

AGE 62

Congratulations! You are now eligible to collect Social Security payments. You may want to think twice before you take this step. But, if you begin collecting Social Security at this early age, your payments may be reduce by up to 30%.

AGE 65

You are now eligible for Medicare. In fact, you can sign up three months prior to your 65th birthday to get coverage that begins during the month you turn 65. This is an important deadline to keep on your calendar, because if you don't sign up right away, your Medicare Part B premiums might permanently increase, and it is possible that you may be denied supplemental coverage. Medicare Part B premiums will increase by 10% for every 12-month period you do not sign up after you become Medicare-eligible. If you are covered by a group health care plan or by a military or veteran's health care plan, talk to your employer or your Department of Defense contact before you sign up for Medicare. In addition, historically, those who were born in 1937 or earlier were eligible to receive full Social Security benefits at age 65. Those born from 1938 to 1942 had their full retirement age rise to between 65 and 2 months to 65 and 10 months. But, as you will see below, those reaching retirement age now have to wait a little longer.

AGE 66

If you were born between the years 1943 to 1954, you are eligible to collect full Social Security payments when you turn 66. If you were born between the years 1955–1959 your full retirement age spans the range between 66 and 2 months to 66 and 10 months.

AGE 67

If you were born in 1960 or later, your Social Security full retirement age is 67. Remember, though, that your payments will increase by 8% per year every year that you delay collecting benefits until age 70.

AGE 70

This is the final year in which you can delay collecting Social security benefits and still receive that 8% annual increase. If you delay collecting benefits past age 70, you will not collect any additional reward—so you may as well start collecting the payments now.

You now must take mandatory distributions from your traditional IRA and 401(k). Talk to your tax advisor about how to calculate the correct amount. This is a critical question, because the tax penalty for failing to withdraw the correct amount is 50% of the amount that you should have withdrawn. So happy (half)-birthday! You now must withdraw some of your hard-earned money. Enjoy it—after all, you are only 70 once.

The Motley Fool is a USA TODAY content partner offering financial news analysis and commentary designed to help people take control of their financial lives. Its content is produced independently of USA TODAY.

St. Marie Financial Advisors, 2014. Important Milestones on the Way to Retirement, February 24, 2014. Retrieved from: http://www.st.mariefinancialadvisors.com.

If you need help or have questions, or want to schedule a free consultation at our office, feel free to contact us at Texas Financial and Retirement, LLC at 903-534-5477 or email questions to bestclients@texasfinancialandretirement.com

DEPARTING DECISIONS

Mortality for humans is 100%. Take the time to address these departing decisions. Complete the attached checklist.

UPDATE YOUR WILL

Determine who will get your assets when you pass. Appoint an executor, executoress, administrator.

This should be kept with your Power of Attorney (see below) and Advanced Directive (see below).

People who should have a copy: Lawyer, You, Power of Attorney (whoever you decide).

DESIGNATE POWER OF ATTORNEY (WHEN NECESSARY)

Gives someone the power to make financial decisions for you, when you are not able to make those decisions for yourself. Ex.: if you are in an accident and are left with no ability to think for yourself.

People who should have a copy: Lawyer, You, Power of Attorney.

FILL OUT ADVANCED DIRECTIVE

Designates your medical wishes.

People who should have a copy: doctor, You, Power of Attorney.

PREPARE A CONTACT LIST

People who should be immediately notified of the death (immediate family, power of attorney, etc.).

People who should be notified and invited to the funeral/memorial.

People who you DO NOT want notified and who are NOT to attend the funeral/memorial.

FINAL EXPENSES PLANNING

Pre-arrange / Plan Service / Pre Pay Service.

Burial / Cremation / Donation to Science.

Where you are to be buried / cremated?

WRITE AN OBITUARY (OPTIONAL)

Allows you to decide what is written.

MAKE A LIST OF IMPORTANT ACCOUNT INFORMATION

All accounts so they can be closed after your death.

Bank | Utilities | Cable | Cell Phone

Where your accounts are (bank, phone, etc.).

Which bank?

Which cable company?

MAKE A LIST OF DEATH BENEFITS & INSURANCE POLICIES

Auto insurance

Home insurance

Life insurance

Veteran services

Social security

MAKE A LIST OF ASSETS

Titles

Registrations

HELP

If you need help or have questions, feel free to contact our office, Texas Financial and Retirement, LLC at 800-675-3227 or email us: bestclients@texasfinancialandretirement.com. You may also schedule a complimentary appointment.

WHAT'S IMPORTANT TO ME / US?

FINANCIAL QUESTIONNAIRE

Name_____Date _____

Living Trust?   ❑ Yes   ❑ No

Home expenses?   ❑ Yes   ❑ No

What are your primary financial concerns?

(List in order of importance)

1. _____ 4. _____

2. _____ 5. _____

3. _____ 6. _____

How would you improve your financial situation if you could? Why?

_____

_____

_____

Special needs or circumstances?

_____

_____

_____

CONFIDENTIAL FINANCIAL OUTLINE

CONFIDENTIAL FINANCIAL OUTLINE

The purpose of this meeting is to gather some basic information about you so that we can reinforce the positive things that you are doing and discover any ways to improve your particular situation. This information is held **confidential** and will **not be released**. Without this information it will be impossible to determine any needs or make any recommendations.

Client Name _____ Nickname _____ DOB _____

Spouse Name _____ Nickname _____ DOB _____

Client -- Retired? _____ Current/Former Occupation _____

Spouse – Retired? _____ Current/Former Occupation _____

Address _____ Email: _____

City _____ State _____ Zip _____

Phone _____ Cell Phone _____

Number of Children _____ Names and Ages _____

_____

_____

Do you have the following?:

Will	Y ____	N ____	Living Trust	Y ____	N ____
Power of Attorney (POA) Assets	Y ____	N ____	Umbrella Liability Insurance	Y ____	N ____
Power of Attorney (POA) Health	Y ____	N ____	Long Term Care Insurance	Y ____	N ____
Children's Names on Your Accounts	Y ____	N ____	Living Will	Y ____	N ____

Assets:

Please bring the following latest statement or the latest summary of assets, ownership and titling:

1. Credit Union/Bank Accounts _____
2. Mutual Funds/Stocks/Bonds _____
3. Brokerage Accounts _____
4. Retirement Accounts from Work _____
5. C.D.s _____
6. Treasury Bills/Savings Bonds _____
7. Annuities _____
8. IRAs/401-Ks/Keoghs/TSAs _____
9. Insurance
   (Life, Long Term Care) _____
10. Promissory Notes/Contract for Deed _____
11. Other Assets _____

Question: **Do you live off the interest your savings/investment dollars earn?**   Yes / No

Real Estate: Home Value $_____   Automobiles and Personal Property: $ _____

Other Real Estate: _____

Business Interests: _____

Taxes:

Please bring in last year's Income Tax return.

(Please Continue on Next Page)

FINANCIAL INFORMATION

Please provide information on all monthly income sources listed below.
Please enter all numbers with NO commas. Totals will automatically calculate.

Client	Spouse
Monthly Salary: $_____	Monthly Salary: $_____
Social Security: $_____	Social Security: $_____
Pension: $_____	Pension: $_____
Investments: $_____	Investments: $_____
Other: $_____	Other: $_____
R.M.D.: $_____	R.M.D.: $_____
Total Monthly: $_____	Total Monthly: $_____

What are your current monthly living expenses? $_____

ECONOMIC IMPACT OF LOSING A SPOUSE

Please enter all numbers with NO commas. Totals will automatically calculate.

Client	Spouse
Amount at risk should _____ die first.	Amount at risk should _____ die first.
Social Security: $_____	Social Security: $_____
Pension: $_____	Pension: $_____
Other: $_____	Other: $_____
Total Monthly at Risk: $_____	Total Monthly at Risk: $_____
"Total at Risk" represents a loss of $_____ per year and a loss of $_____ over 10 years.	"Total at Risk" represents a loss of $_____ per year and a loss of $_____ over 10 years.

RETIREMENT EXPENSES

Name _____   Date _____

Estimate your anticipated retirement expenses

Envision your life in retirement, and think about the expenses you will – or might – incur.
Taking into account your lifestyle and goals, identify which expenses are essential (must have)
to differentiate them from those that are discretionary (nice to have).

Retirement Target Date: _____

Record your estimated monthly retirement expenses and indicate whether it is essential and if it will vary.		AMOUNT ($)		IS IT ESSENTIAL? YES	WILL IT VARY? YES	NOTES
		YOU	SPOUSE			
Housing	Homeowner's Insurance	$	$	☐	☐	
	Household Improvements & Maintenance	$	$	☐	☐	
	Mortgage	$	$	☐	☐	
	Property Tax	$	$	☐	☐	
	Rent/Condo Fees	$	$	☐	☐	
	Other	$	$	☐	☐	
Utilities	Electric	$	$	☐	☐	
	Oil/Gas	$	$	☐	☐	
	Phone/Cable/Internet Fees	$	$	☐	☐	
	Water/Sewer	$	$	☐	☐	
	Other	$	$	☐	☐	
Personal	Clothing	$	$	☐	☐	
	Groceries	$	$	☐	☐	
	Laundry/Dry Cleaning	$	$	☐	☐	
	Personal Care (health & beauty)	$	$	☐	☐	
	Other	$	$	☐	☐	
Health Care & Insurance	Dental, Vision, Hearing	$	$	☐	☐	
	Medical Insurance	$	$	☐	☐	
	Medicare Premiums & Expenses	$	$	☐	☐	
	Medicare Supplemental Premiums	$	$	☐	☐	
	Other (e.g., Out-of-Pocket Pharmacy Costs)	$	$	☐	☐	
	Long-Term Care Insurance Premiums	$	$	☐	☐	
	Disability Insurance	$	$	☐	☐	
	Life Insurance Premiums	$	$	☐	☐	
	SUBTOTAL	$	$			

Record your estimated monthly retirement expenses and indicate whether it is essential and if it will vary.		AMOUNT		IS IT ESSENTIAL?	WILL IT VARY?	NOTES
		YOU	SPOUSE	YES	YES	
Family Care	Support of Children/Grandchildren	$	$	☐	☐	
	Support of Parents	$	$	☐	☐	
	Other Obligations	$	$	☐	☐	
Routine Transportation	Auto Loan/Lease Payments	$	$	☐	☐	
	Excise Tax/Registration Fees	$	$	☐	☐	
	Gasoline	$	$	☐	☐	
	Auto Insurance	$	$	☐	☐	
	Routine Maintenance	$	$	☐	☐	
	Other Commuting Expenses	$	$	☐	☐	
Recreation	Club Memberships	$	$	☐	☐	
	Hobbies	$	$	☐	☐	
	Travel & Vacations	$	$	☐	☐	
	Other	$	$	☐	☐	
Entertainment	Dining Out	$	$	☐	☐	
	Movies/Theater/Sporting Events	$	$	☐	☐	
	Other	$	$	☐	☐	
Charitable Donations And Gifts	Charitable Donations	$	$	☐	☐	
	Gifts	$	$	☐	☐	
Custom Expenses	Expense #1	$	$	☐	☐	
	Expense #2	$	$	☐	☐	
	Expense #3	$	$	☐	☐	
	Expense #4	$	$	☐	☐	
	Expense #5	$	$	☐	☐	
	Expense #6	$	$	☐	☐	
	SUBTOTAL	$	$			
	SUBTOTAL From Page 4	$	$			
	TOTAL	$	$			

AMOUNTS IN BANKS, CREDIT UNIONS AND SAVINGS & LOANS (NON-IRA)
(i.e. Checking, Savings and Money Market)
Please enter all numbers with NO commas. Totals will automatically calculate.

Name of Institution	Type of Account	Maturity Date	Interest Rate	Approximate Balance
1. _____	_____	_____	_____	$ _____
2. _____	_____	_____	_____	$ _____
3. _____	_____	_____	_____	$ _____
4. _____	_____	_____	_____	$ _____
5. _____	_____	_____	_____	$ _____
			TOTAL	$

IRA ACCOUNTS AND OTHER RETIREMENT ACCOUNTS
(Please bring in your latest reports/statements)

Account Type & Location (i.e. Bank, Broker, Employer, etc.)	Type (i.e. 401k, IRA, TSA, etc.)	Approximate Market Value
1. _____	_____	$ _____
2. _____	_____	$ _____
3. _____	_____	$ _____
4. _____	_____	$ _____
	TOTAL	$

STOCKS AND BONDS
(Where you hold the certificates yourself)

Name of Stock or Bond	Number of Shares	Approximate Market Value
1. _____	_____	$ _____
2. _____	_____	$ _____
3. _____	_____	$ _____
4. _____	_____	$ _____
	TOTAL	$

RISK ASSESSMENT QUESTIONNAIRE

The Risk Assessment Questionnaire helps to determine the best asset mix for a financial plan, based on the answers given to the questions below. This page must be completed for compliance purposes.

(Please Only Check One Box For Each Question)

Time Horizon - Your current situation and future income needs.

1. What is your current age?
   - ☐ Less than 45
   - ☐ 45 to 55
   - ☐ 56 to 65
   - ☐ 66 to 75
   - ☐ Older than 75

2. When do you expect to start withdrawing income?
   - ☐ Not for at least 20 years
   - ☐ In 10 to 20 years
   - ☐ In 5 to 10 years
   - ☐ Not now, but within 5 years
   - ☐ Immediately

Long-Term Goals and Expectations - Your views of how an investment should perform over the long term.

3. What is your goal for this investment?
   - ☐ To grow aggressively
   - ☐ To grow significantly
   - ☐ To grow moderately
   - ☐ To grow with caution
   - ☐ To avoid losing money

4. Assuming normal market conditions, what would you expect from this investment over time?
   - ☐ To generally keep pace with the stock market
   - ☐ To slightly trail the stock market, but make a good profit
   - ☐ To trail the stock markets, but make a moderate profit
   - ☐ To have some stability, but make modest profits
   - ☐ To have a high degree of stability, but make small profits

5. Suppose the stock market performs unusually poorly over the next decade, what would you expect from this investment?
   - ☐ To lose money
   - ☐ To make very little or nothing
   - ☐ To make out a little gain
   - ☐ To make a modest gain
   - ☐ To be little affected by what happens in the stock market

Short-Term Risk Attitude - Your attitude toward short-term volatility.

6. Which of these statements would best describe your attitudes about the next three years' performance of this investment?
   - ☐ I don't mind if I lose money
   - ☐ I can tolerate a loss
   - ☐ I can tolerate a small loss
   - ☐ I'd have a hard time tolerating any losses
   - ☐ I need to see at least some return

7. Which of these statements would best describe your attitudes about the next three months' performance of this investment?
   - ☐ Who cares? One calendar quarter means nothing
   - ☐ I wouldn't worry about losses in that time frame.
   - ☐ If I suffered a loss of greater than 10% I'd get concerned.
   - ☐ I can only tolerate small short-term losses.
   - ☐ I'd have a hard time stomaching any losses.

MUTUAL FUNDS AND/OR BROKERAGE ACCOUNTS
(Please bring in your latest reports/statements)
Please enter all numbers with NO commas. Totals will automatically calculate.

Name of Brokerage Firm/Mutual Fund	Number of Shares	Approximate Market Value
1. _____	_____	$ _____
2. _____	_____	$ _____
3. _____	_____	$ _____
4. _____	_____	$ _____
	TOTAL	$

PROMISSORY NOTES & TRUST DEEDS
(Where someone owes or is paying you on a note)

Name of Debtor	Interest Rate	Approximate Balance of Note
1. _____	_____ %	$ _____
2. _____	_____ %	$ _____

RESIDENCE & OTHER REAL ESTATE OWNED
(Use another sheet if more space is needed)

Property Address	Original Cost	Approx. Value	Debt	Net Cash Flow
1. _____	$ _____	$ _____	$ _____	$ _____
2. _____	$ _____	$ _____	$ _____	$ _____
3. _____	$ _____	$ _____	$ _____	$ _____
4. _____	$ _____	$ _____	$ _____	$ _____
5. _____	$ _____	$ _____	$ _____	$ _____

LIMITED OR GENERAL PARTNERSHIPS
Please enter all numbers with NO commas. Totals will automatically calculate.

	Name of Partnership	Type of Investment	Approximate Market Value
1.	_____	_____	$ _____
2.	_____	_____	$ _____
3.	_____	_____	$ _____
4.	_____	_____	$ _____
		TOTAL	$

LIFE INSURANCE
(Please bring in policies and latest statements)

	Company	Name of Insured	Type of Insurance (Whole Life, Term)	Death Benefit	Loan Against?
1.	_____	_____	_____	$ _____	$ _____
2.	_____	_____	_____	$ _____	$ _____
3.	_____	_____	_____	$ _____	$ _____
4.	_____	_____	_____	$ _____	$ _____
			TOTAL	$	$

ANNUITIES
(Please bring in contracts and latest statements)

	Company	Annuitant/Owner	Interest Rate	Approx. Value	Date Purchased
1.	_____	_____	_____ %	$ _____	_____
2.	_____	_____	_____ %	$ _____	_____
3.	_____	_____	_____ %	$ _____	_____
4.	_____	_____	_____ %	$ _____	_____
			TOTAL	$ 0	

OTHER ASSETS

		Approximate Market Value
1.	_____	$ _____
2.	_____	$ _____
3.	_____	$ _____
	TOTAL	$

8